5 STEPS

to a

DRY BASEMENT

or

CRAWL SPACE

Niagara Falls, Prospect Point, New York

*The flow of water over the American side of the falls
was completely stopped during the summer of 1969.*

Ron Gay has written a wonderful book that helps ordinary people understand the mysteries of basements, gutters, and water! His explanations are clear and make sense even to the most uninformed homeowner (including me).

I was fortunate to meet Ron as a neighbor after buying a home with a serious seepage problem. With his help, my panic and frustration were transformed into insights and planning. Ron explained what was happening and why, and what steps could be taken to solve the problem at the source, using well-designed gutters and landscaping instead of costly foundation changes and pumps.

I recommend this book to any current or potential homeowner. You will have an ally as Ron's kind voice guides you through. It will demystify your basement and help you take control of your water problems.

— **Linda Morrison,** *Homeowner*

This is one of those rare books written both for the homeowner and the professional.

For the homeowner, it provides an opportunity to learn about what goes on under and around your house. This book is written to be an easily-referenced resource. If you choose to do the work yourself, it will provide all the necessary information. If you hire the work out, you will become a wiser purchaser of such services and get the best result.

For the professional, it will make a valuable reference manual. It will also make a fine textbook for those learning the trades.

This book will make you a wiser homeowner or professional. It's worth the read.

— **Fred Will,** *Residential Building Contractor*

5 STEPS

to a

DRY BASEMENT

or

CRAWL SPACE

A Guide for
Homeowner & Professional

Also Included:

- Slab Foundations
- All About Gutters
- Mold and Bacteria

Ronald K. Gay

WELKIN HOUSE • PONTIAC, MI

Hear the Welkin Ring

WELKIN HOUSE, Pontiac, Michigan 48341
©2005, Ronald Kenric Gay
All Rights Reserved. Published 2005. First Edition
Printed in the United States of America

DISCLAIMER

Publisher Provided Cataloging-in-Publication Data

Gay, Ron.

5 steps to a dry basement or crawl space : a guide for homeowner & professional : also included, slab foundations, all about gutters, mold and bacteria / Ronald K. Gay.

Pontiac, MI : Welkin House, c2005.

xx, 146 p. : ill. ; cm.

Includes bibliographical references (p.143-144) and index.

ISBN 0-9763652-0-0 (alk. paper)

1. Dampness in basement—Handbooks, manuals, etc. 2. Basements—Handbooks, manuals, etc. 3. Drainage, House—Handbooks, manuals, etc. 4. Waterproofing—Handbooks, manuals, etc. 5. Dwellings—Maintenance and repair—Handbooks, manuals, etc. I. Title.

TH9031 .G39 2004

693.89—ddc22   2004112546

For information, contact:
WELKIN HOUSE
146 W. Lawrence Street
Pontiac, Michigan 48341
248-762-2969
www.welkinhouse.com

Other **WELKIN HOUSE** publications:
House & Home Almanac for Real Estate Professionals
©1993. Ron Gay. Out of print.

For Frances and Walter

*"What does education do?
It makes a straight-cut ditch, of a free, meandering brook."*

Thoreau, Journal 1850, undated

CONTENTS

PART IV • ALL ABOUT GUTTERS

QUICK TROUBLESHOOTING GUIDE

APPENDIXES

GLOSSARY

BIBLIOGRAPHY

INDEX

LIST OF ILLUSTRATIONS

Photographs   Page

Photographs   Page

Drawings

Maps

PREFACE

As a residential building contractor and past home inspector, over the past twenty-five years or so, I've had lots of exposure to houses with wet basements. As a consultant I've evaluated countless homes to advise homeowners specifically on how to solve such problems. Many times I've encountered the attitude that the more money thrown at this problem, in the way of aftermarket waterproofing systems, the faster it will go away. Experience has taught me there is a better way.

My father was a civil engineer and contractor. He initially built structures out of concrete, later turning to underground construction, installing pipelines and pumping stations. In almost all of his projects the transport of water was integral. This is what I was exposed to in my youth, traveling with him from job to job. I'm sure it's why I've focused on basement seepage problems, while working on and inspecting houses.

The years I spent as a home inspector caused me to work hard at knowing the facts so I could inform my customer while increasing my knowledge about building. During those years I was always on the look-out for books that would help me achieve those goals. I've yet to find a comprehensive, well-written book on wet-basement problems. When I wrote and published a reference book on home ownership in 1993 I devoted several pages to wet basements and solutions I had at the time. I was also busy consulting homeowners on the subject with a fairly sophisticated consulting service that included a "20-point" check list.

My Wet-Basement Consulting Service consisted of three appointments and was very successful at solving people's seepage problems. One major goal of my service was to be completely objective, that meant not referring workers to implement my recommendations, and of course, not making the repairs myself. I did, however, provide suggestions on where the client might go to find a good contractor or trade person to make the improvements.

I'm not a big believer in aftermarket waterproofing systems and when I became more knowledgeable about them I was further convinced there is a better way to deal with moisture in basements. I've never recommended a company of this type to solve a seepage problem I was called to help with. From my experience it is rare to find a waterproofing contractor that is well-educated on the exterior maintenance of a house as it pertains to runoff and other sources of water around the home.

There are companies that repair existing weeping tile systems and waterproof basements in a manner consistent with new-construction standards and codes but these types of repairs are rarely needed to stem the flow of common basement seepage.

ACKNOWLEDGMENTS

My sincere thanks to Cheri Gay for her work in editing this text, and for her overall input on book style and presentation. Also, many thanks to Marty Lyle for her dedication in typesetting and layout. Thanks to the Oakland County Health Department, the International Code Council, Ed Wirtschoreck, Margie Leddin, Robert Chapman, Betsey Dexter Dyer, Emily McQuate, Kelly Palm, and Judy Palmer. Special thanks to Mona Parlove for her support and input over these last two years, and the preceding years leading up to this project.

Illustration credits include frontispiece, Welkin House archives; photos throughout text, Ron Gay; additional photos in text, Mona Parlove; septic system drawing by Oakland County Health Department; soil map from U.S. Department of Agriculture; miscellaneous line drawings by Ron Gay and Welkin House archives; photo of the author by James Fassinger.

INTRODUCTION

An average-size house roof generates about 160 gallons of runoff water per hour during a moderate rain.* This is equal to about three fifty-five gallon drums. If certain poor maintenance conditions exist around your home, this water can funnel directly into your basement or crawl space. Most basement seepage occurs during precipitation. The way a house sits on the land, the additions made to the house and yard over the years and the level of maintenance a homeowner keeps are all factors that determine whether or not a coming rain poses a threat to your home. Heavy rains can mean big trouble. Sustained heavy rainfalls can be catastrophic.

Many people are mystified by water that enters their basement or crawl space. The mystery shouldn't be: where is the water coming from, but rather, what changes do I need to make to keep it out? Also important to know: who can I trust to help me with my problem?

Building methods and geology vary around the globe but basements are essentially the same everywhere … masonry boxes built into the ground. So while there may be variations from region to region, country to country, I believe the information here can be applied universally with good results.

My goal in writing this book is to use what I have learned, sharing these successes with a greater audience with the hope of making homes more pleasant and healthy places to live while saving folks some cash along the way. While there is a lot of information included here I've strived for simple and easy-to-understand lessons that can be carried out by the average homeowner. **The 5 Steps** have been set aside so they can be accessed easily. Appendixes are included to give more detailed information for those who desire it. There is a Quick Trouble-Shooting Guide for immediate assistance until **The 5 Steps** can be followed in detail.

The term basement also represents cellars. Crawl-space foundations are included but the emphasis is on basements. Lessons for exterior maintenance apply to the basement and crawl space. Crawl spaces are commonly above ground and therefore have less chance of flooding yet are still prone to problems, like basements, caused by mismanagement of surface water.

Some of the information presented will come at you more than once as I feel it necessary to reinforce my message for this long overlooked and misunderstood subject.

I am a big believer in objectivity and have strived to provide that throughout my years in business. This is one area of home maintenance that I know can lead homeowners to spend thousands of dollars unnecessarily. In this book you will

Source: www.gardenwatersaver.com

not find aftermarket waterproofing systems recommended but instead alternative ways to stem the flow of basement and crawl-space seepage. I also will not refer companies or products by name.

Although there is no shortage of articles written on basement seepage, some by esteemed universities, you will find facts here that have never been observed or disclosed before as they relate to dissolving the myths around basement and crawl space seepage.

At the onset of this book I would like to respectfully challenge all building code councils to consider amending their codes to thoroughly address the installation of gutter and aftermarket waterproofing systems.

The necessity for proper gutter systems is evidenced by the percentage of houses that have installed them and by the high number of homes with basement seepage as a result of defective and improper gutters and downspouts. A certified protocol, coming from a governing body within the building-code industry, would do much in correcting this problem.

As for aftermarket waterproofing, the International Residential Building Code does not specifically address these systems and as a result many products and services are installed without building permits and below inspection standards. The result being, homeowners that are sold waterproofing that may be completely inappropriate for their situation and even a detriment to their home.

PART I

BASIC FACTS

This section provides basic information relating to houses and basements in order to understand the dynamics of foundation seepage. It is not overly technical or involved and sets the stage for The 5 Steps.

- My Experience with Wet Basements
- House Foundations
- The Nature of Concrete
- Protecting Foundations
- Drains & Drain Lines
- Soils
- Water Tables
- Flooding
- Sources of Unwanted Water
- Underground Tunnels

MY EXPERIENCE WITH WET BASEMENTS

My Own Homes

My early childhood was lived in a house with a slab foundation. I didn't relate to basement water problems until later, in our second family home. It was a quad-level built in the 1960s. We experienced minor seepage several years after moving in that was caused by an underground downspout drain pipe.

Through the years I have owned several homes, all older. My experience with those houses varied from no seepage of any kind to minor seepage that was easily corrected by exterior maintenance. I've owned homes built on slabs, crawl spaces and basements and have always tried to keep water away from the foundation, not always in a timely manner I must admit.

Crawl Space Experience

A crawl space is nothing more than a short version of a basement, not habitable. Some crawl spaces are actually too low to crawl through. The house I've owned for many years has a small basement and the rest is crawl space. I know there has been dampness in the crawl space without going down to see. The musty smell tells me. Just having an earthen floor of course can create a musty smell but when water enters the equation the smell is unmistakable. Fortunately my crawl space floor is at grade level so there is never standing water, or the capacity for it because the soil is sand. As a consultant I have seen the full gamut of crawl space conditions, in some cases terribly unhealthy living environments including rotting floor joists.

Consultant & Educator

The first home inspection I performed was in 1985. The home inspection protocol was loose in the early years of that profession. Each home inspector had a different approach to performing his or her service. While performing my very first home inspection I got a lesson from a seasoned Realtor. I was well aware that there was water getting into the basement but it was the Realtor who pointed out the malfunctioning downspout at the corresponding area outside of the basement. It was a lesson I never forgot and it inspired me to look for causes, not merely report conditions.

Because wet basements are so often a bone of contention in real estate transactions I quickly realized that the more I knew about causes and solutions the more I would be able to give a more thorough report to my clients. I didn't really hone my knowledge on the subject until I wrote the reference book, *House & Home Almanac, for Real Estate Professionals,* (WELKIN HOUSE, C. 1993).

Subsequent to writing and publishing that book I began giving workshops on wet basements and providing a consulting service devoted to it. While preparing for both of these new ventures I did more research on the subject that included learning about soil types, flood plains, municipal drain systems and more, so that I would be well informed. I even learned the specifics about the most common aftermarket waterproofing systems in my area. I then designed my curriculum and consulting service armed with this body of knowledge.

I have inspected over two thousand homes from roof to cellar, most often for prospective home buyers. Sometimes they were vacant but most often the homes were occupied. Sometimes sellers were less than forthright on seller disclosure forms when it came to disclosing moisture problems in basements. One owner went so far as to build a false wall in front of a badly-bowed basement wall without disclosing it during the sale. I've consulted scores of individuals specifically on matters relating to basement seepage. In those instances it's been one familiar story over and over.

In all of my travels, inspections and consultations I repeatedly went into homes that had some type of water trouble in the basement or crawl space. Typically when there had been basement *flooding* it was from a backed-up floor drain. This was commonly caused by heavy periods of rain that overloaded the municipal drains at the street, causing floor drains to back up in all, or many of the basements on that street.

Inspecting Homes

During my home inspection routine I would enter the basement, that I always saved for last, walk around the outside walls, look at the floor tile, sump pump and the bottoms of the walls and stairs. In doing so I could quite accurately come up with a history of the basement, or crawl space, in regards to seepage. The most common observation was to look at the corners of the basement walls and see efflorescence, staining and mildew. These locations almost always corresponded with the location of a downspout on the exterior side of the wall. Sometimes the problem was not a downspout but a sunken slab of concrete. In many cases the homeowner thought the downspouts were fine. Too often the homeowner said the gutters and downspouts had been cleaned when they had not.

I don't want to sound overly simplistic, but these are examples of my most typical findings during a home inspection. The results didn't vary when I went on a "wet basement" consultation hired by the homeowners themselves. They claimed they had tried everything and if they had not already spoken to one or more waterproofing contractors then they had names and numbers they were going to call if I could not help.

My Philosophy

It's not fair to say that homeowners knew the answers and had tried those remedies. The truth is, they thought they knew what to do but really didn't have the information or experience to focus on the subtleties that are at the root of the problem. The experience I have enables me to look beyond the obvious and see things such as garden weed barriers that collect water during rains and funnel it into the basement.

Aftermarket waterproofing systems don't keep water away from the basement, instead they encourage it to come in, collect it in a plastic wall panel or drainage pipe buried in the floor that in turn drains into a sump. It is then pumped back outside. My philosophy, consistent with building codes in the construction of new homes, is to manage water on the exterior of the building so that water is kept away from the foundation of the house and therefore out of the basement or crawl space.

If there is a high-water table below the basement floor then work may be needed to restore the original weeping tile system around the *outside* of the foundation wall. But this is rarely necessary for common basement seepage and, I might add, does not ensure against future seepage.

HOUSE FOUNDATIONS

There are three types of house foundations discussed in this book. The main focus of this text is to address houses with wet basements but along with that crawl spaces must be discussed because in many ways they have a greater potential for causing structural problems and toxic indoor environments. Because crawl spaces are out of sight and uninhabited a lot of people aren't as aware of the wetness there compared to a basement where laundry is done, children play and extra space is valued.

Slab foundations have different kinds of problems that are less common and obvious.

Basement Foundation

A basement is a concrete box in the ground that a house is built on. Most houses built before 1900 had basements made of stone and were more often called cellars. After 1900 they were built of concrete block. About 1970 or so poured concrete walls became the more common method for building basements. Wooden basement building also started about this time but never caught on. These are general time periods when these methods were used. Many exceptions exist.

When a modern concrete basement is made a large hole is dug, larger than the size of the intended basement. Then a footing is poured that consists of a concrete pad around the perimeter of the proposed basement. On top of the footing concrete is poured inside forms to create the walls, typically 8" thick, or concrete block walls are laid. Once cured the walls are coated with a tar-like substance on the outside that helps keep the concrete walls dry inside and out, should surface water run down them at any time after the home is completed. This is called damp proofing.

Around the outside base of the wall, just below the basement floor, but not below the level of the footing, a pipe is laid in gravel. The pipe has holes in it and is connected to either a sump in the basement floor, a municipal storm drain line nearby or it may run to a dry well, or to the back of the lot if grade permits. The pipe is covered with more gravel and then the basement is backfilled. This is the weeping tile. The sump in the basement has a pump that pumps collected water back outside or in some cases into the sewer line.

Basements are commonly backfilled with the earth that was removed to dig the hole. Some communities may require sand and/or gravel to be used for backfilling as was done in decades past.

The basement floor is poured at some time during the building process once weather conditions are right and generally after the structure is erected above.

Slab on Grade

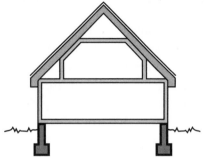

Crawl Space

Quad or Split Level

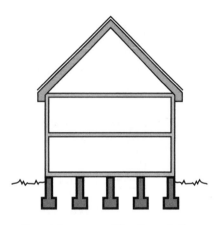

Crawl Space on Pier Foundation

**Shallow Basement or Cellar
with Crawl Space**

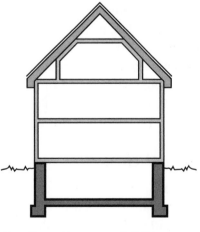

Two-Story House on Full Basement

FOUNDATION TYPES

Crawl Space Foundation

A crawl space foundation is like a very short basement, usually with a dirt floor. Weeping tiles may be installed depending on local codes and the elevation of the crawl floor in relation to grade. Damp proofing may be applied if any or all of the crawl space walls and floor are below grade. Crawl spaces in my area are required to be a minimum height for navigation purposes, about two feet, and have a plastic vapor barrier on the ground that is covered with pea gravel. Vents may also be required, though I don't recommend them.

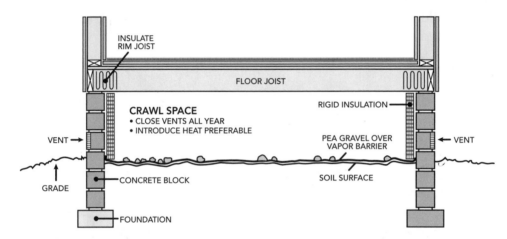

CRAWL SPACE VENTILATION & INSULATION

Slab Foundation

This foundation type is sometimes referred to as a slab-on-grade. This means the level of the slab, or floor, is close to grade level. Slabs are poured on a footing. In this part of Michigan footings need to be 42" deep to avoid frost heave. Vapor barriers beneath the slab prevent moisture from migrating through the concrete into the living space. The slab floor is typically 4" thick but is thicker beneath supporting walls or columns. A weeping tile may be employed if the slab is built in an excessively wet area but typically it is not part of the original construction process.

Split-level House

This house has two or three types of foundations. It may also be called a bi-level, tri-level or quad-level. A quad-level has a basement, a lower level that is only halfway underground and two levels above ground. The tri-level may have a lower level, a slab for the main level and an upper level over the lower level. It can also have a main floor level built over a crawl space rather than a slab. Lower levels, including basements may have heating ducts buried in the concrete slab. This is also a common feature of ranch homes built on slabs during the 1950s and 60s that is discussed in detail in the chapter on slab foundations.

THE NATURE OF CONCRETE

Concrete, in its modern-day formula, has been around about one hundred years. This mixture is hardened with Portland cement, a turn-of-the-century innovation. While this product has made endless opportunities possible for building modern roads, foundations, parking structures, etc. concrete is a very brittle material. Cracks in concrete are common and may affect the structural integrity of a structure such as a bridge, skywalk or basement wall, though, in basements cracks in walls and floors most often *don't* compromise the structural integrity of the building.

When building a house, steps should be taken to prevent and minimize the occurrence of cracks in floors and walls. The variables during construction that affect a successful concrete installation are many and include: temperature; humidity; precipitation; working time; water content of concrete; travel time to job of ready-mix truck; experience of contractors; moisture in ground; soil type; curing period before backfilling; additives that may be used; curing compounds; existence of vapor barrier, gravel or reinforcing wire and steel; and ratios of ingredients or strength of mix.

All of these variables combine to make a sound or failed product with concrete. It may seem daunting to try and get these ingredients just right but with an experienced contractor and cooperative conditions success is usually attained.

A few examples of unsuccessful projects might be: backfilling around basement walls before proper bracing, or curing, causing a wall to fall in; adding too much water to the mixture causing a poor finish on the basement floor, or spider cracks; pouring concrete over soil that is not properly compacted causing settlement of foundation walls or floor.

The point here is to inform homeowners that concrete does crack and it is more common to find concrete walls and floors with cracks than without. **Cracks don't cause basement seepage.** Whether a crack is in a basement floor or wall the crack is merely an entry point for water that has not been properly managed on the exterior of the building. Water that comes up through cracks in basement floors can be from a downspout or other exterior surface-water problem, especially when seepage has been occurring for years. Cracks in walls can be sealed but this won't ensure against water entering the basement from a heavy rain or snow-melt. It may only divert the water from coming in through the crack to another vulnerable place.

The Nature of Concrete

It is possible to seal up a crack from the interior and keep water out of the basement but be aware that if water was coming in before the crack was sealed, and no corrections were made to keep water away from the foundation, then the exterior basement wall will continue to get wet during a heavy rain. It may only be a matter of time before it comes into the basement at some other place like a chimney clean-out or floor crack.

The best way to seal a wall crack is to dig down at the exterior and seal it with an injected silicone or like product or a masonry plaster. But, this should not be necessary if water is kept away from the foundation.

PROTECTING FOUNDATIONS

Does anyone think that the black stuff applied to basements of new houses, before they are backfilled with dirt, provides waterproof protection for the basement? If you said yes you are probably like most people. That's what I thought years ago before all of my experience and research in this area. The fact is this thin membrane of sealant provides damp proofing only, *not waterproofing*. The difference is comparable to a water-repellent jacket that resists moisture under some conditions but when it comes to downpours won't keep you dry. You have to get the fully-waterproof jacket to keep rain from penetrating to your clothes.

Damp Proofing

Like the water-repellent garment, damp proofing keeps moisture out in some conditions. This thin coat of tar-like material applied over the concrete wall of a |new basement may initially seal any minor cracks or rod holes, (holes left by the rods from concrete forms after they have been removed), but after the basement walls have fully cured and dirt has been filled in around them conditions will be tested. New cracks may form, or existing ones widen, that are no longer bridged by the sealant. Rod holes may have been so lightly coated that any static water against the wall may seep through.

I've inspected enough *new* homes to know that they can easily have basement seepage if the grading is incomplete or gutters have not been installed.

A builder's warranty against such moisture problems may cover repairs for a number of years but likely not the cost of damaged carpeting or belongings. Even if damaged belongings are covered it is a real headache to experience this kind of problem, especially in a new home.

Waterproofing

Waterproofing on the other hand, strictly as it applies to new houses, is a more complete application of a substance or a system designed to keep the basement dry under virtually all types of wet conditions. There are numerous ways to achieve this including heavy applications of asphalt-like materials that seal the footing and wall joint as well as all of the wall surfaces. There are products designed to go against the concrete wall that will channel water down to the weeping tile while protecting the wall itself from contact with water. Any of these bona fide systems should be approved by a local building code authority.

Protecting Foundations

There are even double weeping tile systems that keep ground water from rising up through the basement floor. For instance, a house built on land with a high water table that is near or just below the basement floor level may be required to have weeping tile around the outside of the basement wall footing and also on the interior of the basement at the footing. These two drainage lines act in unison to keep ground water out of the basement. In a house without this threat the weeping tile is typically installed on the exterior of the foundation only.

New basement with damp proofing protection on walls.

Effects

The vast majority of new and existing homes today have not been waterproofed but damp proofed. This will be adequate if the exterior of the house and property are maintained properly but if not, seepage can occur. It would be easy to build every house so that water would not penetrate the basement or crawl space under the most severe conditions but this adds cost. Even in decades past, cost was a critical component for a builder to be competitive. The waterproofed basement is uncommon. If a house has been waterproofed it usually means that the site the house is built on is more prone to heavy concentrations of ground water rising up from beneath or around the basement walls. So while waterproofing is an extra measure above standard building practices, it is critical that it be done well, or under extremely wet conditions flooding may occur.

This is a simplified explanation of these two methods. They have a like function in building a home, that is to protect the foundation from wetness and most importantly keep water out of the living space of the home.

This is a good time to point out how these two building techniques support my philosophy on wet basements. I believe that the foundation of the house should be kept dry at all costs, or as dry as possible. Waterproofing and damp proofing are designed to achieve this goal. This is the correct way to build a house and, in my view, the only correct way to maintain a house. Many aftermarket waterproofing systems actually encourage water to enter a basement through the wall to be collected in a drain pipe under the floor that in turn drains into a sump. I believe this goes against good building practices.

Other Variations

There are some measures that fall between damp proofing and waterproofing such as adding 6-mil polyethylene over the tar coating on the newly-built foundation, or possibly an ice and water shield product, typically used on roofs — see the manufacturer before applying a product of this type.

One should also know the distinction between damp proofing, waterproofing and aftermarket waterproofing. In this region of the country the term, "basement waterproofing," is generic in meaning but typically is used by homeowners to describe aftermarket waterproofing. Aftermarket waterproofing is different from methods used for new construction. Because this distinction is so important I have addressed it in a dedicated chapter.

DRAINS AND DRAIN LINES

Types

There are two types of drainage lines for most houses with basement and crawl space foundations. The sanitary sewer carries waste water from sinks, tubs, toilets and washing machines and is connected to either a city sewer line or a septic system. In urban and suburban settings the floor drains in basements and laundry areas are usually connected to the sanitary sewer while in rural houses with septic systems the drain may run to a dry well.

The other drain type is the weeping tile, that is installed while the basement is being built. It is laid into the ground all the way around the basement just below the level of the basement floor. In many urban and suburban locations this drain is connected to a municipal drain at the street. Typically in older urban neighborhoods the downspouts of houses were also originally connected to these lines via a cast iron or glazed crock that stuck up out of the ground for the downspout to connect to.

In some cases when the weeping tile is not connected to a municipal drain line the drainage may run off to the back of a sloping rural lot or into a sump in the basement that in turn pumps the water back outside to the surface or into an underground drain line that runs to a ditch or even into a dry well.

Often the municipal sanitary sewer and weeping tile drain lines from the house come together in one common drain at the street. If there are storm drains at the curbs these also empty into this main drain. In other communities the sewage is kept separate from surface water collection drain lines.

The International Code Council (ICC) does allow houses to be built without weeping tile. In these cases the house must be built on soil comprised of sand and/or gravel.

Underground Downspout Drains

I have always advised clients to not use the old urban underground drain lines for the downspouts as they are no longer reliable, possibly causing basement seepage. Communities in metropolitan Detroit have also recommended disconnecting from these so that rain water will not overload the burdened metropolitan drain system. All water that runs into systems that combine rain water with sewage ends up in the sewage treatment plants. Having rain water go into a combined sanitary/surface water drain is a major waste of resources. It also results, in some of our communities, in an overflowing system during times of heavy rain. This sends untreated sewage spewing into our lakes and rivers sickening and killing wildlife and posing major health risks for people.

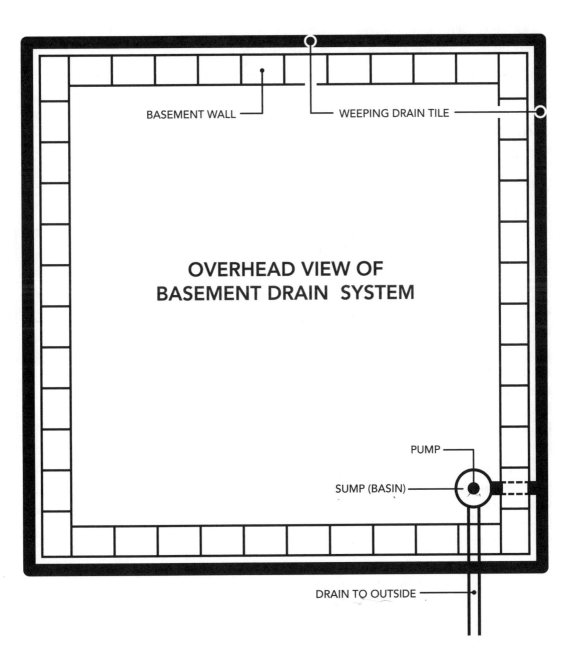

BASEMENT WALL

WEEPING DRAIN TILE

**OVERHEAD VIEW OF
BASEMENT DRAIN SYSTEM**

PUMP

SUMP (BASIN)

DRAIN TO OUTSIDE

Overhead view of basement with weeping tile and sump pump.

Other underground downspout drain lines installed ten, twenty or more years ago need close scrutiny to judge their function.

New versions of underground drains for downspouts may be perfectly viable if installed and maintained properly.

Maintenance of Drains

The sanitary drain line of a house, or sewer, can be cleaned periodically as needed. The weeping tile system, in older homes, usually cannot be snaked or cleaned because of the crude method in which the drain tiles are laid, combined with sand and gravel plugging the line.

To say that damaged weeping tile is the cause of basement seepage is not truly correct. Except for basements built on high water tables the weeping tile is merely a back-up system to divert surface water from coming into the basement. During my home inspection days I would often inspect brand new homes. It wasn't unusual to find some basement seepage occurring before the house was even occupied yet it had a new, functioning weeping tile and sump pump. This demonstrates that fixing weeping tile or adding interior drain systems is not the answer to the problem of drying up a basement with surface-water seepage.

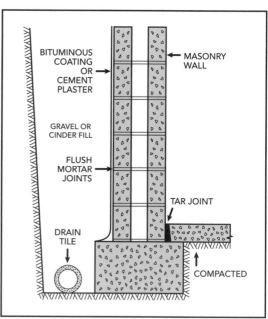

Detail of basement wall, floor and weeping tile.

My office is located within an old house that was built before weeping tiles were used. If my gutters are clean and functioning I have zero seepage under the worst conditions. The foundation walls of this house are fieldstone and limestone mortar, an old-fashion soft mortar. These walls have withstood the test of time without gutters or weeping tile for well over a century and a half. This indicates how houses built on sand, without weeping tile, can survive without seepage and without damage to the foundation.

SOILS

The Spectrum of Soils

An important contrast between different regions of the country is the geology, more specifically, soil types and terrain. In Michigan there are vast differences even in the same county. Northern Michigan is mostly sand but close by, areas with wetlands and lakes have clay that forms lake bottoms.

In the county where I live there is an area to the south that used to be wetlands many years ago and as such has a clay subsoil that does not allow water to percolate down into the ground quickly after a hard rain. The property where I have my office in the north end of the county is all sand. It's a real challenge to keep up with watering the garden during the hot summer months. And yet the quad-level house where I grew up is built on high ground that is the hardest clay I've yet to find.

Clay and sand are as different as two soils can be. Clay is hard and dense and does not allow water to seep through it while sand acts as a sieve encouraging water to filter through at a rapid rate. These are the extremes for soil types around basement foundations. Other types of soil fall between them when it comes to porosity and absorption capability.

Effects On Houses

The way soil types affect basement seepage and proper runoff of surface water from the roof or yard is important when solving seepage problems but it is not the determining factor.

The area in the south part of my county I spoke about is notorious for wet basements as well as bowed basement walls. The reason for this is that poorly managed water coming off of roofs, driveways and patios becomes more of a problem for these houses with poorly absorbing sub soils. The water runs along the basement walls and sits there. It has lots of time to find its way into the basement through the most vulnerable places like cracks, wall and floor joints, chimney cleanouts, etc. At some point through the years this static water sitting outside the basement wall may freeze, in turn cracking and bowing the basement wall at the frost line. Bowed and cracked walls can also be caused by clay soil around the foundation becoming wet and expanding, especially when the house is new.

In the case of my property the sandy soil allows for the runoff from roofs and yard to seep quickly into the ground well below the depth of the basement floor. Although my yard is sandy the potential for basement seepage still exists, and I might add has occurred.

Soils

The importance of discussing soil types is to explain how they relate to problems with water entering basements and crawl spaces and to stress that no soil type ensures against this problem. Obviously, if seepage can occur in houses with sand around the basement walls as well as with clay, then any soil that falls between these two types, such as sandy loam or loamy clay, can also allow seepage to occur. The main difference is that a soil like clay can greatly inhibit the absorption of water through the ground and in doing so make a basement much more prone to heavy seepage than the example with sand.

Therefore a basement built in sand that lacks a gutter or downspout extension may experience some mild seepage in very heavy rain while the house with clay soil can experience heavy seepage in mild rains. You don't have to know what type of soil lies against your house foundation to keep water from entering the basement. But it is important to know that certain soils can demand extra diligence in keeping the foundation dry.

Building Techniques

It's interesting that some houses are built with sand and gravel backfilled around basements for the purpose of letting runoff water filter quickly into the ground below, past the level of the basement floor or crawl space. While there is no way of knowing which houses were built using this technique the lessons to come will illustrate that while this is a benefit to any house it is not necessary to prevent basement seepage.

In contrast to this builders will commonly backfill around the basement walls with the earth that was dug to make the hole. If clay comes out, clay goes back. As a result water may not filter down along the basement wall to the weeping tile quickly. The result is increased risk of seepage. So again the preventive measure is to keep water away.

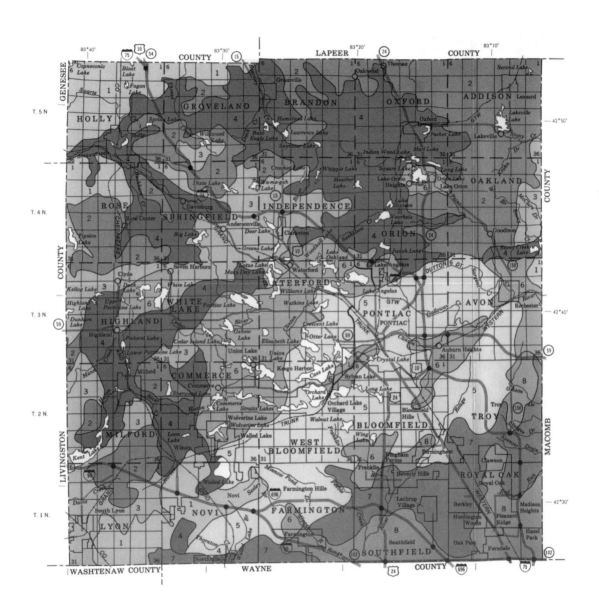

Part of a soil map showing various soil types, indicated by shaded areas.
Source: Soil Survey of Oakland County, Michigan. U.S. Department of Agriculture.

WATER TABLES

There are three types of water tables to know about in this quest to prevent basement seepage. They all refer to a level of water below the ground. Two are most common and relevant.

Apparent Water Table

This is the common water table we all think about that is nothing more than the level of water that appears upon digging a hole. An example: go to a vacant lot, dig a test hole of any size diameter, the depth of the hole at which water appears is the apparent water table. It represents a thick zone of free water in the soil, or completely saturated soil at a given level.

Apparent water tables fluctuate with the seasons and amounts of precipitation. That is why a sump pump may run often during warm months and infrequently in winter.

Perched Water Table

A perched table is a level of water in the ground that is separated by a dry or unsaturated layer of soil below it. Perched water tables are created around a house when surface water, runoff from downspouts for instance, runs down the outside of a basement wall but can go no farther because of clay sub-soil. As a result the water sits along the basement wall until it can find someplace to go, often inside the basement.

Artesian Water Table

This third type is unique in that it is under pressure. Much like an oil well gushes to the surface, when an impermeable layer of soil or rock is penetrated, an artesian water table rushes or blasts to the surface. This is also a type of hydrostatic pressure.

The artesian water table is not a factor in existing houses with problems in their basements or crawls. The other two are important to know in determining where the water is coming from, as will be discussed.

Effects on Houses

A water table that lies below a basement floor can rise *sometime after* heavy rains, or during very prolonged periods of rain, and cause sump pumps to run more often. If water enters a basement during or immediately after a normal rain it's likely surface water. If the house was built before modern building codes and mechanical systems, say pre-1920 or 30 when sumps came into use, the house should not have a high water table and almost conclusively has a surface water problem. There are cases when a house was built when the water table was well below the basement floor, but over many years, say a decade, or maybe a century, the table has risen to the point of entering the basement of an old house. In these cases a historic house would experience severe flooding without much relief from dry weather.

Houses across the nation vary infinitely from one another. They are built by many builders, in various types of geography over different periods in time, and exhibit endless examples of abnormal or unusual building methods and situations. So there will be exceptions to the common rules I have laid out here. Consequently one of these puzzles may be hard to solve by a homeowner alone.

I have found this to be one of the main challenges in understanding existing older homes. The inconsistencies and unknowns can be great. Factor in changes made without permits and projects done by unqualified homeowners, or contractors, through the years and you realize just how evasive some problems can be to solve.

Water tables combined with soil types determine if a piece of land is suitable for building and what type of foundation is necessary. If the water table is well below the level of a basement floor then a house with a basement may be built with a simple weeping tile.

If the water table is at or near the level of the basement floor then surely a sump pump will be needed along with a weeping tile — some local governments may require sump pumps in all basements. An interior and exterior weeping tile may also be needed. If the ground is extremely wet with a water table near the surface then it is possible that only a house on a crawl space or slab will be allowed. If the soil is incapable of supporting a conventional foundation then maybe no house at all will be permissible. If the home is in a flood plain or high-tide, area codes may require building on stilts, well above the ground.

These conditions greatly affect the types of experiences homeowners will have with a home in regard to basement seepage problems. In some houses I've inspected there was a high-water table because the house was located near a river or lake. As a result some houses had two sump pumps. The pumps could not only run at the same time as needed but one could serve as insurance should the other cease to operate. This is necessary because of the constant high flow of water into the pump basin, or sump.

FLOODING

Flood Plains

If the banks of a river overflow a flood occurs. If a basement floor drain backs up a flooded basement results.

A flood plain, designated as such by the Federal Emergency Management Agency (FEMA) for a specific locality, is an area of land at risk of flooding from a known source of past floods such as a lake or river. These are low-lying areas, especially near wetlands. If a house lies within a flood plain then additional homeowner's insurance is necessary to insure against flooding. It's not always clear on how being in a flood plain affects conditions beneath the ground.

As mentioned, water tables under the ground can vary based on levels of precipitation and runoff from neighboring lands. If a house is in a low-lying area and drainage ditches, for example, aren't maintained and functioning properly then the ground may become too saturated to handle any surface water runoff. Although standing water can constitute a flood it may not meet the definition of a flood plain if it is temporary pooling caused by melting snow or a heavy downpour, or a blocked or slowly-draining ditch.

Yard Flooding

If a home's yard is extremely low causing water to stand after moderate to heavy precipitation and the property is not in a flood plain then the solution will likely require changes to the grade on the entire lot or part of it. If the property is within a flood plain no remedy may be available. Though, if in a flood plain, the damage resulting from a flooded basement or crawl space may have claims paid through flood insurance.

Basement Flooding

Basements are flooded when seepage enters through walls and floor, the sump pump fails or a floor drain backs up. Where I live a backed-up floor drain is most common in post-war suburban communities that have streets with curbs and storm drains. When prolonged heavy rains occur the streets are deluged with runoff. The drains at the street curb, carrying rain water away, become overloaded and start to back up in the streets and eventually in the basements of the houses on the street.

This kind of problem has nothing to do with the adequacy of the drain lines of the individual homes. It is entirely a problem of the local municipality's main drain lines and system. In the communities near me residents not only experience flooded basements but vast amounts of sewage overflow from waste-water treatment plants that occasionally spills into lakes and rivers. A new drain system is being created to deal with this problem. A basement can also become flooded as a result of seepage, seepage from surface water. When there is a high amount of water in the basement homeowners tend to become so unnerved they think it must be a major and expensive problem. They don't realize how easy it is for high volumes of rain coming off roofs or patios for instance, to be funneled directly into the basement due to improper outside maintenance.

It's obvious that basements can also flood from a failed sump pump, or frozen or plugged sump pump discharge line.

Crawl-space Flooding

The floor of a crawl space is often at grade level. For this reason we know that standing water in these cases can only be from surface water. Attending to it by the methods set out here will be productive. However, if the land around the house foundation with a crawl space is in a flood plain or very low yard, that invites pooling of rain, then these remedies may prove unhelpful.

If a basement floods from a failed sump pump we know the solution immediately. If a floor drain backs up from a flooded street curb, past experience and neighbors let us know what has happened. But if flooding is from surface water finding its way into the basement we often become confounded and panicked. This book will help you differentiate and find solutions.

SOURCES OF UNWANTED WATER

Backed-up floor drains aside, the water that gets into a basement comes from the surface or beneath the ground, the surface or beneath the ground, the surface or beneath the ground. There is no other source, it's that simple.

Surface Water

Surface water comes from runoff after rains and melting snow. The highest concentrations of surface water for homes is off of roofs and paved areas. The area of a roof collects immense amounts of water during precipitation, about 160 gallons per hour for an average-sized roof. The purpose of a gutter system is to manage this water, protecting the house and its occupants. Driveways, patios, sidewalks and concrete porches are other collection areas for rain. How these areas are constructed and maintained will determine whether rain water runs away from the house, or towards it, that may then run into the basement or crawl.

Ground Water

Ground water comes from beneath the ground such as a high water table or an underground spring. I consulted a homeowner with a house that had an underground spring, that fed a nearby river, that had changed direction since they purchased the house many years before. The result was a steady flow of underground water near one of her basement walls. Technically this is not a high water table but an underground spring, nevertheless it still is ground water. Where I live basement seepage from high water tables, or ground water, rarely causes common basement seepage. If a house has a high water table and the sump pump malfunctions you have instant flooding. Otherwise things are fine. So typically it's either flood or no problem at all with this kind of water source, but not seepage after a rain.

Hydrostatic Pressure

One of the terms often used by aftermarket waterproofing contractors, in selling a homeowner a waterproofing system, is the term hydrostatic pressure. This is nothing more than water trapped between a basement floor or wall and the earth, that creates enough static pressure to force itself into the basement. Labeling a basement seepage problem as hydrostatic pressure is sidestepping the issue. The right approach is to keep water from running down the wall or beneath the floor in the first place by following maintenance guidelines set out in this book.

Common Conditions

The importance of distinguishing between surface and ground water is to take away the mystery of where water comes from that seeps into a basement or crawl space. The previously mentioned experience about the underground spring is the only case I can recall where a homeowner had water problems caused by ground water. Of the thousands of homes I thoroughly evaluated, the problems I discovered were otherwise related to surface water. It's not to say that I didn't inspect homes with high water tables, especially in areas close to lakes and rivers, but they were maintained with sump pumps, some homes had two.

Surface water was also the culprit for people considering aftermarket water-proofing systems when I consulted them.

The problem experienced by the great majority of those reading this book is caused by surface water. This is a very manageable condition and with the exception of possibly replacing a slab or two of concrete, inexpensive to address.

To recap, surface water comes from the surface while ground water comes from under the ground. Surface water can usually be easily managed, ground water is more difficult, but rarely do conditions change beneath the ground after a house is built to necessitate expensive repairs to the house's weeping tile.

One further point. It is possible for a house with a high water table to have seepage problems caused by surface water. The homeowner with a known high water table is at a disadvantage. For it is easy to become overly focused on that fact and in doing so completely ignore the symptoms of seepage directly caused by surface water. For that reason I strongly urge *all homeowners* to take this path of addressing surface water problems before turning to high water table questions.

UNDERGROUND TUNNELS

When I gave workshops for homeowners, and consulted with them privately on how to correct basement seepage I used several teaching aids. One of them looked like an ant farm, two pieces of glass stood up on edge, with sand in between. If you've seen the toy ant farm like this you'll recall how the ants live between the clear panels digging tunnels throughout the maze of sand.

This maze of tunnels exists behind basement walls that have had seepage of any kind over the years, or just dampness.

Underground tunnels against basement walls — envision your basement wall being made of glass and seeing through it just like the ant farm — have been formed from years of surface water seeping or running down the outside of a basement during moderate to heavy rains. They are carved out by water finding its way from the surface to an opening in the basement that may be a crack in the basement wall, a rod hole, the joint where the basement wall meets the floor, a chimney clean-out, etc.

These tunnels clearly illustrate the importance of keeping water away from the house foundation walls. If water gets anywhere near the wall it will find these tunnels, that act like a plumbing pipe, supplying water directly to the inside of your home. When it rains it's like turning on a faucet. It takes no time for the water to travel from the top of the ground to the interior of your basement.

I see no practical need to try and eliminate these tunnels. Instead, like all of our other examples, we need to keep water away from the house, from entering these underground tunnels. In the following chapters I will demonstrate how to keep water at bay for long-term, and hopefully an indefinite period of time.

PART II
THE FIVE STEPS

These pages deal specifically with identifying and correcting conditions that are causing foundation seepage in the basement or crawl space of your home.

- **Step 1**   Describe Existing Problem
- **Step 2**   Inspecting Your Home
- **Step 3**   Correct Roof Runoff
- **Step 4**   Correct Landscaping
- **Step 5**   Correct Sumps, Drains, Cracks
- Case Studies

STEP 1:
DESCRIBE EXISTING PROBLEM

Getting Started

NOTE: *One problem that cannot be prevented by making changes to the features of one's home is the flooding of a basement caused by a backed up floor drain, directly resulting from an overburdened municipal drain. For example: You live in a neighborhood with paved streets and curbs. During a heavy, extended rainfall storm drains at the street, that are also connected to the sanitary sewer and basement floor drains, are overloaded and cannot drain fast enough. A common result when this happens is that basements of the houses on the street have water that backs up at the basement floor drain. This flooding has nothing to do with the condition of the house, the house exterior or mechanical systems. It is a municipal matter that can only be resolved by improving the capacity of the municipal drain system as it services your community. It may be possible to put some type of plug in your floor drain to prevent back up. In doing so you will also prevent it from draining water that enters the basement from another source such as an overflowing washing machine or broken water line.*

Consult your local building authority regarding the use of plugs in floor drains and whether claims can be made against damages resulting from overburdened municipal drain systems.

This part of the book is where the work is done to solve your seepage problem. If you read Part I then you have a basic understanding of the elements of a home that relate to this condition. Having these fundamentals will make this part of the book easier to apply to your own situation. Although this book is not a workbook it is written with the goal of the reader implementing the methods and materials described and recommended. This chapter starts the process of focusing on your particular problem, or problems as is often the case, with a wet basement or crawl space.

There are several questions to answer that will help solve your particular water problem, such as how long have you lived in this house? How long has the condition persisted? If it hasn't been ongoing what changed around your house that may signal the cause of it?

Step 1: Describe Existing Problem

Create A Report

Right now I want a clear description of the problem you are experiencing in your basement or crawl space.

Start by titling your spiral notebook, ***Basement and/or Crawl-Space Evaluation***, whichever applies.

Include your name, address, date.

Note on the first page which direction the house faces. This will allow you to designate which corner of the basement is a problem. For instance, northeast corner of basement has seepage.

Date each entry throughout this notebook. Organize this part by way of worst problem first. Label it ***Problem Number One***. Then describe what the problem is. Where is it located in the house? When does it occur? How do you suspect it happens? Make notes about what the problem area corresponds to on the house exterior. For example: seepage in N.E. corner of basement occurs during heavy rains only and location of seepage corresponds with patio outside basement wall. Be as specific as possible on every aspect of this report such as: water backs up at floor drain during heavy rains but no sewage smell is apparent, and sinks, tubs and toilets are otherwise draining.

Also stipulate if the basement is finished or unfinished. How much is finished? Some walls? Ceiling? Designate which walls again by north or south wall.

Can you actually see the water coming in? Describe how many times this has happened in the past year or if over many years, try and determine if it happens during mild or moderate rains or just in heavy extended downpours.

What about in spring thaws? Does it only happen in March or April? Is there always a snow pile on that side of the house during that time of year?

Describe the area at the inside of the basement or crawl where the seepage exists. Is it at the base of the floor? Only at a wall crack? Do you have water coming in at the chimney clean-out near the basement floor?

For those experiencing serious flooding where water covers the entire floor it may be more difficult to trace a source to a west wall or corner. Does water come up through cracks in the floor?

There are many basements with more than one source of water coming in. Some houses have several areas where seepage enters that varies with the amount of rainfall. It may be difficult to remember if the conditions relate to whether the gutters were clean when the last occurrence took place or if someone left the garden hose or spigot running. Sprinklers are also a source for water coming into the house.

Here are the things you will need:

1. lined 8.5"x11" spiral notebook with holes for a 3-ring binder
2. a few sheets of graph paper 8.5"x11" or larger
3. camera with a roll of 24 exposures
4. 3-ring binder with pockets at front and back covers
5. some clear 3-ring plastic sleeves to hold photos and graph paper
6. rain gear

I know because growing up in a quad-level house we had sprinkler lines that leaked against the lower-level foundation wall. It wasn't obvious from the outside of the house and inside it was such a small amount of water that it went unseen for weeks or months under carpeting.

Again if you can make a connection between the water's point of entry to a corresponding exterior feature, such as a downspout, then note: "Seepage enters on southwest corner of basement during moderate to heavy rains. Location corresponds to a downspout on the exterior of the house."

Common basement seepage coming in at both walls in a corner.

Suspected Source of Water

I want to distinguish again between water that enters a basement or crawl space coming from the surface versus water that comes from below or within the ground, a high water table. Although a high water table can be affected by rain in moderate to heavy amounts it is unlikely a rainy day will have an immediate effect on water levels below the ground. So by observing the exact conditions when seepage occurs it will help to distinguish seepage that comes from surface water versus ground water.

Generally speaking if a basement has a flooding problem that is not linked to an immediate rainfall, but instead is caused by a sump pump failure or a delayed response to heavy rain days before, then the problem may be from ground water or a high water table. Beware also of water that comes up through cracks in the basement floor. It is not necessarily from ground water just because it comes up through the floor. Surface water can easily find its way down a basement wall and beneath the footing and floor. It will then come in at the first opportunity, such as a floor crack.

Step 1: Describe Existing Problem

Make It Clear

I want you to document everything you can that relates to this seepage or water problem. Although no one else has to review this report I think it is best to make it clear and well-organized for future reference, and also in case someone else might have to review your work it will be legible and sensible. You will also have it when you sell your home. If a home inspector reports signs of past basement seepage you can show the report and relate that the problem has been remedied.

You'll get great satisfaction after correcting this nuisance especially when you go back over this document and see what conditions were that you have since fixed.

The documentation of your problem is also the basis for the inspection report forthcoming. All of this will go into your notebook and will be a bonafide inspection and report on your home as it relates to foundation seepage and exterior maintenance conditions. This serves another purpose. It will change the way you look at your home forever by enabling you to focus on maintenance defects that were cloudy and difficult to understand before going through this process.

Seepage in this basement is coming in at wall, floor and chimney clean-outs.

STEP 2:
INSPECTING YOUR HOME

This process is simple. It is an item by item look at exterior features of the home that relate to basement seepage. If you follow it closely and make a good report results should prove successful.

Whenever I did a consultation for basement seepage I didn't just look at the spot where seepage occurred. I took the opportunity to perform a complete inspection to reveal any lurking improprieties and to eliminate the possibility of a new problem arising down the road. For this reason you will perform a complete inspection of your home as it relates to water problems in the basement or crawl space. It is only after the inspection and correction processes are complete that you will return to your problem as described in the first part of your report. You will then be able to make the correlation between what the problem was and what corrections were made that correspond with that location or issue.

Using the graph paper draw a footprint of your house noting which direction the house front faces. This is an aerial view of your home's outline on its lot. It is not important to make this footprint drawing too detailed. It should reflect the shape of the house walls. The roof lines can also be included. The scale of the drawing should allow plenty of room for notes around the four sides of the graph paper. Items that will be noted include problems with: downspouts, adjoining hard surfaces, weed barrier areas, planters, sprinklers.

❧ You will also be taking photographs of every side of the house. For larger houses more than one photo may be necessary for a side. Shots from house corners showing two sides in one shot may be helpful. Close-up photos of major defects should also be included. A twenty-four exposure roll should be adequate.

We are going to use a list of items for the sake of inspection that will be used again in the following chapters as they pertain to corrections. All items will not apply to one house. The ones that do apply should be included on the footprint drawing and in the photos taken.

Inspection Begins

The following inspection protocol is broken down using numbers and letters. Use them when writing down your own conditions. Place an NA next to any item that does not apply. For example:

IA1. no, yes

IA2. metal

IA3. some loose

IA4. yes

IA5. no

IA6. no, one open end

You can elaborate further in your answers as you wish.

Step 2: Inspecting Your Home

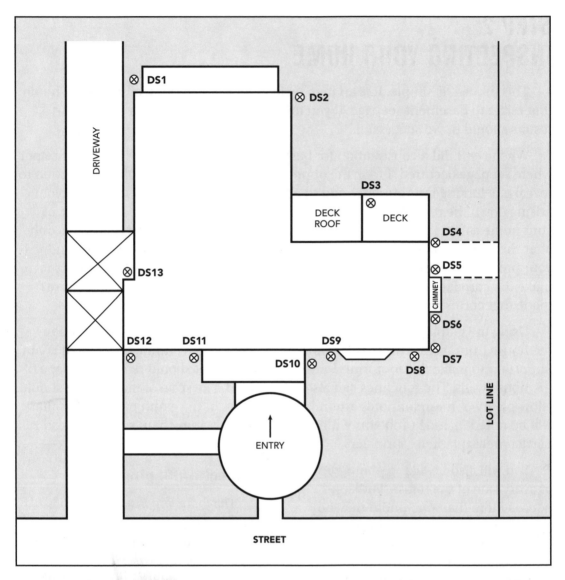

This is a site plan drawn to advise a homeowner on exterior maintenance relating to their basement seepage problems. The X in a circle symbol denotes downspout locations. The numbers correspond to comments on a consultation report. The large Xs denote slabs of concrete at the driveway that had sunken and were in need of replacement or raising. This house footprint, or aerial view was not drawn to scale but merely to represent the shape of the house on the lot and locations of downspouts and problem areas.

I. Inspect Roof Runoff

Roof runoff is the water that comes off of a house roof during rain or snow. We will assume that the house being inspected has gutters and this inspection pertains to those matters. For houses without gutters read each entry before going on.

Start by labeling all downspout locations on the house drawing. Give them a letter or number. You can use a legend or code that is noted on the drawing to indicate references to downspouts as well as other notations to come. So for downspouts, for instance, you can draw a circle with a DS in it and add a number to the side: DS1.

I A. Gutters

A1. Are there gutters all the way around the house? Partial gutters?

A2. Are they metal or plastic? If metal are they half-round or the typical gutter shape, called K-style? K-style gutters are either 4" or 5", 5" being newer, size 4" now obsolete. Measure across top of gutter to determine size.

Cutaway of a K-style gutter.

Half-round galvanized gutter hung with straps. Notice downspout outlet gap at gutter bottom.

Step 2: Inspecting Your Home

The upper gutter on this roof, between the windows, has come loose and will overflow during rain.

A3. Are the gutters secured well to house eave, or fascia?

A4. Do they slope towards downspouts? (An easy way to determine if a gutter slopes to downspout is to stand back in the yard and look at the fascia board that the gutter is attached to. Look at the amount of fascia board exposed beneath the gutter and it will tell you which way the gutter is sloping.)

Gutter splash guard located at roof valley.

Look closely and notice the gutter's right end is sagging. It will overflow during rain.

Tree needs severe trimming away from roof.

A5. At the roof valleys, where two perpendicular roof surfaces intersect there should be a splash guard at the gutter, an inside 90' angle. Is there?

A6. Are gutters capped at the ends, as opposed to an open end where water runs out?

A7. Are gutter joints leaky?

A8. Are there gutter covers or screens?

A9. How many trees are overhead and how close are they to the roof?

I B. Downspouts

B1. On average, there should be one down-spout for every 35' of gutter. Are there adequate downspouts?

B2. Are downspouts located in the best place such as at house corners instead of in the center of a wall? Or are they located in a place that can allow runoff away from the house?

B3. Are there any screens inside the gutters where the downspouts are attached at the outlets, designed to collect debris?

The downspout is located over an old, obsolete underground drain crock. The crock should be filled with concrete at the top. The downspout extension, though screwed on, is not inserted far enough over the elbow.

Step 2: Inspecting Your Home

Downspout running into a brittle and broken, obsolete underground drain line.

B4. Are downspout parts inserted into one another properly, male into female from top to bottom?

B5. Are downspout parts screwed or riveted together?

B6. Are they secured to the wall with straps?

B7. Are any downpouts connected to underground drains?

B8. If so, where do the underground drains terminate?

B9. What is the height of the downspout elbow from the ground?

B10. Is there an extension on each downspout elbow? How long?

This homeowner avoids too much water in the rear yard by running a downspout along left house wall to front. This is not recommended unless PVC pipe is used and is cemented together.

**The location of this downspout, in the center of the wall, is improper.
It should be located at a corner to facilitate effective runoff away from foundation.**

B11. What kind of splash block, if any, does the downspout empty onto?

B12. Is the ground sloped away from the house where the downspout splash block empties?

B13. Are there roots, trees or shrubs impeding the slope away from the house?

B14. For downspouts that empty onto hard surfaces such as drives, walks, patios, etc. are these surfaces sloping away from the house?

Step 2: Inspecting Your Home

**Some homeowners perfer to install their splash blocks backwards
to avoid washing out flower beds. This is a recipe for basement seepage
or damp walls at least.**

This downspout is emptying onto a backward sloping plastic splash block.

Step 2: Inspecting Your Home

Corrugated hose can get knocked off. Ridges in hose also collect debris causing slow flowing runoff or backup.

This downspout emptying next to the foundation has created a low spot.

Step 2: Inspecting Your Home

**Downspout extension is unnecesarily long. Grade appears low
and no splash block in sight.**

**A condominium front yard with several downspouts emptying into a flat or
low area. This illustrates poor planning by the builder and/or developer.**

Improper downspout due to low grade, no extension at elbow and splash block is plastic instead of concrete.

Downspout extensions are way too long. The grade is too low. Both downspouts should be reconfigured to empty side by side or one relocated.

Step 2: Inspecting Your Home

Both downspouts are improperly extended. They lack proper slope,
grade is low and there should be extensions on the elbows that rest on
concrete splash blocks, not these plastic types.

Improper downspout and sump extensions. They are both too long,
lack proper slope and splash blocks.

Step 2: Inspecting Your Home

Two downspouts empty into a small area at the
basement exterior wall. The grade is low, there are
no downspout extensions or splash blocks.
Basement seepage can be expected.

An antiquated underground
downspout drain which is
unreliable.

I C. Debris

C1. Are the gutters clean of debris?

C2. Are the downspouts clean of debris?

C3. Are underground drain lines free of debris?

C4. Do the gutters and downspouts function properly during a heavy downpour? Using a hose to simulate rain isn't the best test.

An improper splash block has no sides.
The downspout should also be extended.

II. Inspect Landscaping

II A. Hard Surfaces

A1. Do driveways, sidewalks, patios, porches slope well away from the house?

A2. Does a neighbor's driveway direct a lot of water close to your house foundation?

A3. Is there an old patio under a deck near the house? Does this patio slope away from the house?

A4. Is there a stretch of driveway that cannot be raised or replaced to direct water away from the house due to the surrounding grade of the yard or adjoining slabs of concrete?

Sunken slab at downspout is two problems, sure to cause trouble.

The entire driveway along side this house is sunken, combined with two downspouts emtying here is an invitation to heavy basement seepage.

II B. Landscape Features

B1. Do any flower beds within ten feet of the house have either plastic sheeting or mesh fabric weed barriers?

B2. Do spigots have a splash block beneath them, sloped away?

B3. Are there planter boxes or flower-bed edging that inhibit downspout runoff?

B4. Are there any very low areas in the yard within thirty feet of the house that pool during moderate to heavy rain?

B5. Is there a drainage ditch at the house front, side or rear that does not drain?

The front yard of this house was surrounded with gravel on top of plastic weed barrier. Basement seepage was experienced as a result. All of the gravel and plastic must be removed to eliminate the problem.

Black plastic, seen here, is commonly used in flower beds beneath mulch and stone to prevent weeds. When used in this manner, within ten feet of a house foundation, it has been found to cause, or contribute to, basement seepage.

This see-through fabric is also used to keep weeds out of flower beds. Although it is supposed to let water pass through it, from precipitation or watering, it is extremely prone to clogging, and overload due to high volumes of water. The risk for basement seepage is equally great when using this type of weed barrier.

Step 2: Inspecting Your Home

**This downspout empties into a low area that creates a
high risk for basement seepage. It is also improperly extended
with a plastic folding tray and lacks a splash block.**

II C. Stoop With Basement
(see glossary)

C1. Is there an uncovered front or rear porch that has a basement under it? If so
how large is the concrete surface? Does it slope away or towards the house?

C2. Is there edging or planter boxes around the porch at the yard?

II D. Shrubs & Trees

D1. Are there any tree or shrub roots close to the house that prevent downspout
runoff from continuing away from the house?

D2. Are there any roots that prevent runoff of a hard surface like a drive or patio?

II E. Sprinkler System

E1. Are there underground sprinklers against or close to the house? Do they spray away from the house?

E2. Are they free of leaks and functioning properly?

E3. Are the sprinklers set at a moderate frequency and duration of time?

E4. Are there any weed barriers in areas within ten feet of the house where sprinklers run?

II F. Window & Door Wells

F1. Does the house have any window wells or door wells at the foundation wall for basement windows or doors that extend below grade? If so, how old are they?

F2. Do the window wells have concrete bottoms or earthen? If concrete, is there a drain in the bottom of each one? Do they function?

F3. If there is a door well is there a floor drain at the bottom? Does it function?

II G. Septic System

G1. How old is the system?

G2. Was it installed with a building permit?

G3. How close is it to the house?

G4. Has it been inspected for function lately?

G5. Is the soil type likely to be saturated due to the systems age?

G6. Does the lay of the land encourage saturated soil between the septic system and the house?

G7. Do nearby drainage ditches add to saturation of soil at the yard?

G8. How much roof runoff runs to the yard at septic field location?

G9. Do any underground downspout drains run into or through the septic field area that may be malfunctioning or broken?

III. Inspect Sumps, Drains, Cracks

III A. Sump

A1. How old is the sump pump?

A2. Does it work well consistently?

A3. Does it have a check valve to prevent water from running back into the sump after the pump shuts off?

A4. A high-water alarm to warn when the water in the sump is in danger of flooding the basement?

Basement sump pump with lid off is unsafe!

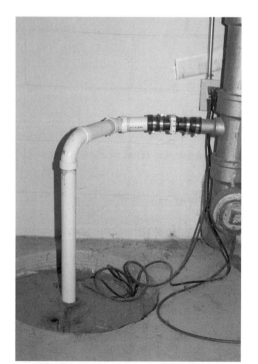

Basement sump with lid on. Notice pump empties into sanitary drain line. This may not be allowed in certain locations. Check valve is between black sections on drain line.

A5. A back-up battery or municipal water-powered system to power the sump pump in times of power outages?

A6. Does it discharge underground or above ground?

A7. If underground what is the destination of drain line?

A8. If above ground is the pipe extended with a splash block? How far is it extended? Does this pipe ever freeze?

III B. Drains

B1. How many floor drains are in the basement?

B2. Do they drain when water runs into them?

B3. Do the floor drains run to the sanitary sewer, a sump or to a dry well?

B4. Is there a sewer line to the city or septic near the house that could be leaking?

III C. Cracks

C1. What are basement walls made of?

C2. Does the basement have any vertical or horizontal wall cracks? Describe each crack by size and location, hairline, less than a quarter inch, more than a quarter inch?

C3. Are any of these cracks apparent at the exterior of the foundation?

C4. Are there any exterior cracks that are not visible at the interior, possibly because of finished walls?

C5. Describe any bowed walls that exist by which wall, location on wall, length of bow, distance of bow out from straight part of wall.

C6. How many floor cracks? Describe by size.

C7. Are there signs of staining or past seepage at any of the wall or floor cracks?

C8. Are there rod holes that show signs of past seepage?

III D. Chimney Clean-outs

D1. Are there any chimney clean-outs in the basement?

D2. Are there signs of seepage from them?

D3. What do they correspond with on the house exterior, such as a downspout, patio, garden weed barrier, planter box, underground downspout drain?

III E. Other

E1. Does the basement, or lower level in the case of split-level house, have any heat ducts within the concrete floor?

E2. If so is there ever a smell that comes from them that corresponds with times of precipitation?

Vertical crack in concrete block wall.

Rod holes on a newly-poured concrete wall.

STEP 3
CORRECT ROOF RUNOFF

All of the following items correspond in assigned number/letter with those in the inspection section.

I A. Gutters

Gutters are not mandated by building codes, though some guidelines are provided in the International Code Council's Residential Plumbing Code on the size of gutters as related to annual precipitation for a geographic region.

A1. Install gutters at all roof eaves that runoff onto yard above a basement, crawl space foundation or problematic slab-on-grade foundation. Roofs on bay windows or porches may be left without if they are extremely small. Partial house gutters may be acceptable provided the areas where gutters are omitted are at parts of the structure with no adjacent basement or crawl space. Damaged gutters should be replaced. Gutters that are 4" across the top should be replaced with 5" K-style. Professional installation of new gutters and repairs is recommended. Be sure and specify seamless gutters. Hanger types include nail and feral, screw and feral, inside gutter bracket with nail or screw, strap around gutter that nails to roof.

A2. K-style gutters are the recommended type. If other types are already in place, and function well under all conditions, do not replace them. Inspect them during a heavy rain. A K gutter can be hung using a few different hanger types. The standard method for hanging gutters is using a long gutter nail and spacer tube, feral. The gutter needs holes drilled on the front edge for the nail to go through. The feral goes on the inside of the gutter with the nail running through it. A gutter screw and feral can be used instead of a nail. An easier and better-looking method is the fastening bracket that goes inside the gutter and screws to the fascia from the inside of the gutter leaving the gutter face free of any nail or screw heads. When fascias are slanted or designed in a way that gutters cannot be nailed onto them a strap may be used that wraps around the gutter and fastens to the top of the roof. When fastened to the top of the roof shingles the nail heads should be touched up with roof cement. It may be difficult to install the strap beneath the shingles without removing them.

A3. Make sure all existing gutters are secured well and are tight to the fascia, and not hung too far below the edge of the shingles. The gutter should be tight up to the shingle on the high end if possible.

A4. Correct any gutters that are not sloping towards downspouts. New-style hangers that fit inside gutters and screw to fascia can be used for minor adjustments. View gutter from a distance and observe the space below it on the fascia board to determine proper pitch.

A5. Install splash guards at inside 90° gutter junctures, below roof valleys, and any where else an overflowing gutter exists or is likely to exist.

A6. Install caps at any gutter that is open-ended. The gutter may have to be removed for this. They are typically on upper roofs. Once caps are in place, install a downspout outlet in the bottom of the gutter and if room, a downspout pipe and elbow or just an elbow if space is limited. Upper-roof gutters with open ends are more likely to cause roof leaks than basement seepage.

A7. Leaky gutter joints can be sealed with a metal mending sealer that comes in a small tube. If the gutters on your house are made up of many short sections, many joints, it might be time to replace them with seamless, professionally installed gutters.

A8. Gutter screens are recommended to keep debris out. This is a heavy-gauge hardware screen securely attached to the gutter and at the roof. I don't recommend adding gutter covers. If they already exist leave them in place unless basement seepage is being experienced in that area. Remove them only after all other corrections have been made and seepage is still occurring.

A9. Trees should be trimmed as high off the roof as possible. If it is aesthetically pleasing to have them low on the roof be sure they are well out of reach of the gutters and shingles.

I B. Downspouts

B1. Add downspouts if there are fewer than one for every 35 feet of gutter. For extremely large expanses of roof every 25-30'. The downspout can also be increased to a larger size.

B2. Re-locate downspouts that fall in the center of the house wall, if possible, to a corner. Sometimes downspouts can be re-located so they discharge at a better place and runoff will stand a better chance of staying away from the house. See a professional gutter installer about re-configuring gutters and re-locating any downspouts that are troublesome, such as from one end of the gutter to the other, so that it is farthest from the house foundation. Sometimes it's as simple as locating a downspout from one end of a gutter to the opposite end. It may be possible to do this without replacing the gutter but instead patching the old downspout hole and re-hanging the gutter to slant the other way.

Step 3: Correct Roof Runoff

House on left has downspout properly located at outside corner of porch gutter. House on right has downspout poorly located next to house which makes it harder to get runoff far from foundation.

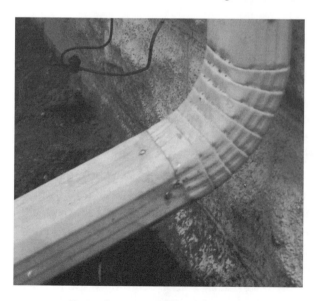

Properly connected and screwed downspout elbow and extension.

B3. Correct any downspout parts that do not fit male into female from the top down.

B4. Screw or rivet all downspout parts together.

B5. Repair loose straps or add new straps to secure all downspouts to the wall. Nail or screw to wood. Use anchors and screws for masonry.

B6. Secure all downspout connections at underground drain pipes. Flush out or repair all underground drains not working. Dig up and replace if problems are found. For suspected problems disconnect and extend with a downspout extension and splash block as listed here.

Downspout strapped to house wall.

B7. Adjust all downspouts that empty onto ground so that the elbow is about 12" above grade before an extension is added. To adjust height, remove elbow and cut with a hack saw or saber saw. To lengthen, screw or rivet a short piece of downspout material to the existing pipe. Reattach elbow.

B8. Add an 18" extension to all downspouts that empty onto ground. The extension should be made of downspout material. Be sure elbow is inserted well into extension pipe. Screw or rivet together. An extension may be left off if the elbow spills onto a hard surface i.e. driveway, patio or walkway and the hard surface pitches

Downspout elbow height should be about 12" above grade.

well away from the house foundation. Be cautious in cold climates not to create an ice hazard in these instances. There are situations when existing landscaping or house features prevents a simple downspout installation as described. There are times when a long extension pipe is required to get the water to an area that slopes away from the house. These extensions should not be made with downspout pipe but instead rigid PVC. There must be a positive draining slope to these long extensions and they must never back up at the downspout connection. PVC pipe should be cemented together.

Step 3: Correct Roof Runoff

B9. Purchase concrete splash blocks for all downspouts that empty onto ground. Provide solid ground beneath each one making sure that the splash block is sloping well away from the house and that the ground around the splash block is also sloping well away from the house. Garden edging and weed barriers should be removed. Use small stones at base of splash block to help disperse runoff. It's also a good idea to place splash blocks on shredded mulch and keep grass away to discourage lawn mowers from coming too close to splash blocks. As mentioned, it's perfectly o.k. to have a downspout, with or without an extension, empty onto a driveway or patio, however, keep in mind this can pose an ice hazard for cold climates. Any extension in this circumstance shouldn't cause a trip hazard.

Downspout running into a corrugated underground drain line.

B10. Remove any trees or shrubs with root systems that prevent runoff from splash blocks.

B11. Remove and replace any hard surface such as driveways, patios, sidewalks that slope towards the house where downspouts empty onto them. Use mud jacking to raise sunken slabs.

I C. Debris

C1. Clean all gutters of leaves and debris, first by hand and then with a hose and nozzle. It's best to wear a mask when cleaning gutters and downspouts to prevent symptoms from mold and bacteria found in the decomposing leaves and twigs.

Downspout running into a PVC underground drain line.

Step 3: Correct Roof Runoff

C2. Remove any device in the gutter that is designed to trap debris preventing it from getting into downspouts. They keep debris out of downspouts but get clogged and cause gutter to overflow. Run a hose with a nozzle attached full force inside all downspouts until it is certain they are completely free of debris.

C3. You can try the hose method for underground downspout drain lines but this method probably won't be effective on blockage that has accumulated over a long time. A professional drain cleaner can likely free up stubborn clogs.

C4. Observe all gutters and downspouts during a heavy rain. Simulating this with a hose on the roof is not adequate.

The downspout in the corner runs beneath this porch slab. It should be fairly easy to determine if it is functioning well or has a clog or break by running lots of water through it from the gutter.

Downspouts run underground to avoid ice problems on this Michigan sidewalk.

STEP 4
CORRECT LANDSCAPING

II A. Hard Surfaces

A1. Replace all hard surfaces that do not slope well away from house. A garden hose can help determine low spots at driveways and patios. Concrete slabs can be raised using a technique call mud jacking. Search the Internet. Slabs that are badly broken should be replaced.

This parking area is paved with open concrete pavers that allow rain to be absorbed into soil.

A2. Neighboring driveways may not be changeable but it might be possible to run a pipe or shallow trench along one to divert the water to the front or back yard and away from your foundation.

A3. Decks constructed over old patios should be opened up to see if the patio slopes towards the house, if it does it may be causing seepage. Save this task as a last resort. If all other corrections have been made per this text and seepage remains a problem at this area the patio will have to be removed, leaving earth in its place.

A4. Sometimes it is possible to add a curb of concrete or asphalt on top of the driveway that will direct water farther down the driveway until it is away from the house foundation.

II B. Landscape Features

B1. Remove all plastic or mesh weed barriers from within ten feet of the house. There are no exceptions here.

B2. Place a 24" square patio stone beneath all outside spigots. Make sure it is tight against the house and slopes well downward.

B3. Remove all flower bed edging that inhibits runoff from downspouts, sidewalks, patios etc.

This planter attached to the house is a problem when the gutter overflows into it.

B4. Raise the grade of any yard area within ten feet of the house that collects water during any rainfall.

B5. Improve all drainage ditches around the house site that do not drain during rainfall. Contact local government authorities.

II C. Stoops With Basements

C1. Uncovered front or rear stoops that have basements beneath them pose a special problem. When it rains the water runs off the stoop and down the side. With no gutter system to collect this runoff the only place left for it to go is down the basement wall in this area. It is possible to install a weeping tile around these stoops that channels the runoff away from the house. Dig a shallow trench, one to two feet deep. Line it with pea gravel. Lay a perforated pipe or hose around stoop walls and extend it away from the house to a low spot in the yard or to a dry well ten to twenty feet from the house.

II D. Shrubs & Trees

D1. Remove, relocate or replant any tree or shrub with roots that inhibit proper runoff of downspouts or hard surfaces such as a driveway or patio.

Step 4: Correct Landscaping

GAY'S DOWNSPOUT EXTENSION METHOD

**Downspout elbow is about 12" above grade. An 18–24" extension is attached with
screws or rivets to elbow. Extension rests on concrete splash block.
Ground is sloped well away from house foundation.**

Step 4: Correct Landscaping

GAY'S DOWNSPOUT EXTENSION METHOD

**Stones are placed at base of splash block to help disperse runoff and prevent washing out of bed. Mulch placed beneath splash block and around area to prevent mowers from getting too close and disturbing extension.
Overall distance about four feet.**

Step 4: Correct Landscaping

II E. Sprinkler System

E1. Adjust any underground sprinklers close to the house so they spray away from the house.

E2. Repair all leaks at sprinkler heads and lines.

E3. Adjust sprinkler frequency and duration to a modest level. If in doubt shorten it dramatically and then increase it back to a minimal amount.

Sprinkler located close to basement outside wall could pose problems.

II F. Window & Door Wells

F1. Install window wells at basement windows only if the grade needs raising around windows to facilitate proper runoff from downspouts or if a very low condition exists causing pooling of water during rainfall that might enter through these windows.

F2. Window wells with concrete bottoms that do not have drains either need the concrete taken out or drains installed. Concrete will have to be taken out to install drains in most cases so it's easiest to just take out the concrete and forget replacing the drain. This will allow rainfall to be absorbed into the soil and should not cause seepage. Window-well covers can be used but often the covers can cause problems

A window well for a basement egress window. Also notice the sump pump drain pipe sticking through the wall. It will need a proper extension and splash block when the yard is landscaped.

by creating a concentration of water running off instead of into the wells that in turn soaks evenly into the ground.

F3. For door wells it is not desirable to have an earthen floor where people come and go into the basement. Therefore, the drain must be repaired, or if missing one should be installed.

II G. Septic System

G1. Determine the age of the septic system.

G2. If the home is a cottage, cabin, old farm house, or built-by-owner it may be that the septic system is not bona-fide and may need replacing.

G3. Check with local health department to determine if septic system meets modern criteria for distance from house.

G4. Have system inspected if not done in last three years. This is especially important for older systems and very old homesteads.

G5. Determine if the soil above a septic field remains saturated, while other areas in the yard have dried out after a heavy rain. If it does remain saturated have the septic system inspected.

G6. Determine if the yard grade between septic and house encourages runoff or pooling. Major regrading may be necessary to the entire yard if pooling exists close to the house and/or a new septic system.

G7. Check with local authorities to improve any adjacent drainage ditches that are causing septic field to remain saturated.

G8. Re-direct any roof runoff that is causing a saturated septic system. Underground drain lines may be an option provided they don't run through or near the septic field area.

G9. Make changes to downspouts and underground downspout drains to divert all water away from septic field area.

STEP 5
CORRECT SUMPS, DRAINS, CRACKS

III A. Sump

A1. Replace any sump pump fifteen years old or older. Recommend pumps that are sealed to the home interior, venting to the outside.

A2. Replace any sump pump that has any erratic function or that has seized, even if it may not be in immediate need.

A3. Install a check valve on discharge line if missing.

A4. Install a high-water alarm if none present.

A5. Install a battery or municipal-water powered back-up system. See a plumber.

A6. If sump pump discharge line empties onto ground be sure it is extended like downspouts using an extension pipe and splash block. If underground, make sure it is leak-free and flowing freely. It may be necessary to dig line up and reinstall it to assure proper function. If pipe is known to freeze it may only function emptying onto ground or into a line buried deeply enough to avoid freezing.

III B. Drains

B1. Make sure all basement floor drains are unobstructed by belongings or structural elements. All drains should have covers that are free of debris.

B2. Have a drain cleaning professional address any drains that are not draining freely.

B3. Install a plug in any drain that is a problem from back-ups at city curbs during heavy downpours. Keep in mind that these drain plugs will prevent water from draining out of the basement if a washer should overflow or a water line breaks.

B4. If there is any smell of sewage when water enters the basement or any suspected leak of a sewer line or septic line that egresses the basement, collect a sample and have the local government health department test it for sewage. Proceed to a professional drain cleaning company in either case, reporting health department findings to them.

III C. Cracks

C1. Clean any efflorescence, mold, dirt, peeling paint, etc. from basement walls. See the *Appendix F* for mold removal.

C2. It should not be necessary to seal basement wall cracks to prevent seepage, however, cracks can be filled with a masonry caulk or silicone sealant in order to prepare the wall for painting. Sealing cracks can also prevent radon from entering the home. Cracks can also be repaired from the outside by digging down the length of the crack and then filling it with materials mentioned. This will not assure against seepage but it will help keep water out of the basement if a gutter or downspout should malfunction.

C3. Interior cracks that are over a quarter inch may be filled with mortar or hydronic cement, a masonry patching cement. Hairline cracks may be bridged by a good masonry primer and paint. Use environmental-quality paints.

C4. Exterior cracks can be filled as described above.

C5. Exterior cracks, not visible at the interior for whatever reason, can be filled at the exterior, again only as insurance against a future failed gutter or downspout.

C6. Bowed walls are not uncommon in basements that have trouble keeping water out and away. They typically occur either right after a home has been built as a result of poor construction methods or within a few years, after mismanaged water is allowed to sit against the outside of the basement wall. Frost or soil expansion causes pressure against the wall that causes it to crack or bow. The question is: when is a bowed wall at risk of falling in? This can only be determined by a structural engineer or architect. Even then it may require months, or even years, of monitoring to determine if it's still moving. Commonly, bowed walls move once and never again. A bow does not make it structurally unsound, unsafe or inadequate. Home inspectors or aftermarket basement waterproofers do not have a unique ability to make this determination.

C7. Floor cracks are easy places for common basement seepage from surface water to enter. It does not mean that seepage is caused by a high water table just because it comes in through the floor. Sealing floor cracks, like wall cracks, can keep radon out and humidity as well. It can also provide some insurance against a future malfunctioning gutter or downspout.

C8. Larger floor cracks can be filled with cement.

C9. Pay extra attention when sealing wall or floor cracks with signs of previous seepage.

C10. Rod holes, left in poured-concrete walls can allow surface water to seep into a basement if not sealed well. Like cracks they can be sealed from the interior and/or exterior. Sealing them from the exterior will be more reliable but rod holes, because they are limited in size, can be sealed well from the interior alone.

III D. Chimney Clean-outs

D1. Chimney clean-outs should be kept clean of all ashes. Be sure door fits and will close.

D2. Signs of seepage from clean-outs will necessitate paying close attention to the exterior of the house in this area. There are no changes to the clean-out that will prevent this problem. Seepage entering through a clean-out is more evidence that the condition is caused by surface water running down the basement wall and into the basement at the first opportunity. The exterior defect, causing surface water to run down the basement wall, is not necessarily right outside a clean-out, or chimney. It may be at a corner of the house with a malfunctioning downspout, for instance, that runs underground the length of the basement wall to the clean-out.

D3. Directly outside the chimney, possible sources of surface water seepage include: downspouts, sunken concrete slabs or brick patios, planter boxes preventing runoff, underground downspout drains, septic systems combined with any of the above, garden weed barriers, sprinklers, faucet, etc.

III E. Other

E1. Underground heat ducts in lower-levels or basements are prone to seepage entering from surface water improperly managed outside the home. As with chimney clean-outs and all other entry points for water into basements these items must be considered, not as the cause of seepage, but as a symptom. If all the exterior maintenance guidelines are followed and seepage still exists it could be a high water table causing the problem. If a working sump pump exists, it doesn't rule out a surface-water or ground-water problem. Surface water may still get into ducts even with a functioning sump pump. If the water table is high and the weeping tile becomes plugged a sump pump might still be operating even though water is getting into underground heat ducts.

E2. Sewage odors emanating from ducts after a rain are an indication that the septic system is in need of inspection and possible replacement. If the house has city sewers it may have a broken line that again will require inspection by a professional drain cleaning company.

CASE STUDIES

The following consultations are first-hand experiences of mine as a consultant for basement-seepage problems. They were performed over a period of about ten years.

Case 1 / Lots of Money Saved

This homeowner described to me the classic case of water being mismanaged at the house's exterior. Their basement was nicely finished. The husband was a retired executive who prided himself in proper upkeep of their home. I was told that they were at their wits end about a seepage problem and were about to call a basement waterproofing company.

It was on the front wall of the house, right of the entry, that water was entering during moderate to heavy rains. I looked at the downspout to the right of the front door and saw that it had a flexible plastic extension hose on the elbow at the ground. When I looked more closely I saw that the extension was not slanted downward so that water would run away from the house instead it was slanted slightly towards the house. This is a perfect example of the homeowner thinking that downspouts and gutters are fine but lack the diligence or proper instruction to look more closely. When I brought it to the homeowner's attention he felt silly. He corrected it and the seepage stopped.

Case 2 / The Quad-Level

This involves a quad-level house with seepage from several sources. Upon my initial evaluation I discovered that virtually all of the downspouts were mismanaged, a large sidewalk at the front of the house was sunken and carrying water towards the house foundation. One of the downspouts was connected to an underground downspout drain.

After I submitted my findings and report the homeowners were instructed to make the corrections and call me to inspect those repairs. When I was called to return it was after some periods of rain. I inspected the changes that I recommended and found some done properly and others not. The homeowners told me that they were still experiencing seepage in the front lower levels but the other areas had subsided. I went back over the changes that had not been made and stressed digging up the underground downspout drain to verify its function.

The homeowner called me back after a heavy rain to explain to me that the seepage had subsided in all but the first lower level. This lower level had heat ducts under or within the concrete slab floor. Not only was there some seepage into these

Case Studies

ducts but a sewage smell as well. It was then I asked about their septic system and proceeded to walk around the front yard. I observed the drainage ditch at the street and walked down the street to see how and where this ditch ran.

I discovered that the ditch farther down the street was totally blocked and this would cause other ditches on the street to have standing water during heavy rains. This was confirmed by the homeowner. They told me their septic field was original and still insisted that the underground drain was fine.

My conclusion was that a combination of a saturated septic field and a front yard that did not drain was causing the ground to be unable to handle any runoff from roofs, at least in the front yard, and as a result the runoff backed up into the underground heat ducts. I still felt strongly that the underground downspout drain was a contributing factor but the homeowner refused to consider my recommendation in that area. I instructed the homeowner to call the county road commission or drain commission to see about getting the ditch on the street draining properly. After that if they were still experiencing problems they should consult a septic expert and investigate the possibilities of connecting to the city sewer system as the conditions of their property might not meet current septic field absorption standards.

Case 3 / Running Spigot & Weed Barrier

During a home inspection I performed I found signs of seepage coming in the front of the house at the basement wall, a rod hole or minor crack as I recall. The inspection was at the request of a potential buyer. The homeowner was present and the house was virtually new. While going over my inspection report with my client I pointed this out. When we were done the buyers presented this concern to the homeowner. They informed us that the spigot had been left running in this location by one of their kids and since that time they experienced some seepage during moderate to heavy rains.

I went outside to give this area a closer look. There was a space between the house and driveway a foot or two wide where this spigot was. The area was covered with stones and when I looked closer I observed that there was weed barrier beneath the stones. Weed barrier is either plastic sheeting or mesh fabric that is used to keep weeds from growing in beds and planters. The problem with this product is that it forms pockets very easily that collect water during rains and inevitably will cause rain water to puddle and run towards the foundation of the house, causing seepage.

I concluded that this was the cause of the problem in this case but there was another side effect. When water runs down a foundation wall for any period of time an underground tunnel is carved out by the water flowing down the wall. If a basement with seepage problems had a see-through wall you could see that underground tunnels exist next to the wall carrying water from the surface down the foundation wall. This is what happened when someone left the spigot running. It carved out a tunnel down the outside of the basement wall and every time it rained thereafter water collected in the weed barrier and found its way down that tunnel into the basement.

I advised the owners to remove the weed barrier. The buyers were satisfied with my diagnosis and never reported any further problem.

Case 4 / Just A Weed Barrier

As in the previous case, this home inspection client experienced some seepage on a basement wall that had stones over mesh weed barrier. Once they removed the weed barrier, upon my recommendation, their problem ceased completely. The mesh weed barrier is designed to let water pass through it but in moderate and heavy rains cannot handle the task. The mesh also becomes clogged with silt over time and therefore is not recommended in any area or bed that is within ten feet of the house.

Case 5 / Lots of Sloping Concrete

This house was for sale for a long time, at least partly because of the evidence of constant water problems in the basement. Upon my inspection I observed that the house was virtually surrounded with concrete walks and slabs that were sunken and carrying rain water towards the house. In conjunction with this the downspouts needed attention and there were some old underground municipal downspout drain lines that were still being used. After these corrections were made the problem subsided.

Case 6 / No Weeping Tile

One house that I owned was so old that it was built before the use of underground weeping tile around the basement. When I first bought the house there were no gutters and I wasn't experiencing any seepage in the basement. After a few years some seepage began coming in one corner after heavy rains. When I installed a gutter at a valley, with a properly extended downspout the problem was solved immediately.

Case 7 / Broken Underground Drain

A lady was getting ready to sell her house but had continued seepage in one corner of her basement. I consulted with her and closely examined the exterior of her house. I saw no obvious problem except an underground downspout drain whose location I couldn't identify. I asked her about it and she was also unsure if it

Case Studies

ran along the area where the seepage came in. She contacted her son and he dug up the drain and found that it ran along the wall right at the point of the problem and was in fact broken right at that location. So with a little time and digging the problem was solved with no real expense.

Case 8 / Lady Gets Sick

One day I got a call from an older lady who complained of an odor in her basement. She lived alone. Her children were adults with families. She expressed to me her despair over her children's refusal to believe her complaint.

She called me as a basement consultant. When I arrived I detected an odor I couldn't identify. When I entered her basement it was quite strong. She had not complained of any seepage problem or backed-up drain, just an odor.

She also explained that she had a septic system and that the problem began after an additive was poured into the septic tank, to assist sewage break down.

I found nothing out of the ordinary in the basement. It was a full basement that had few to no belongings in it and showed no signs of seepage yet some efflorescence on the walls. On the exterior of the house the feature I focused on was underground downspout drains. All of the rear downspouts were connected to pipes that drained underground and somewhere to the far rear of the lot. It was an older system and very suspect. It was a ranch-style house with a large roof area. This meant that large volumes of water went through these underground downspout drain lines.

Though there was no way for me to check the function of the underground drain pipes I felt I had all the evidence I needed with the facts given to me by the homeowner. Everything she told me was credible and articulate. With that information, combined with my own nose's detection, I made a diagnosis.

Somewhere in the backyard an underground downspout drain line, or lines, was leaking badly during rains. When this happened it mixed with the chemically-treated sewage from the septic field nearby and somehow collected along the exterior basement wall. It was enough dampness against the outside of the wall to cause this chemical smell to penetrate into the basement interior. I will add that there were signs of dampness on the basement walls, meaning water was against the outside of the wall at certain times, it just never entered by way of seepage.

The sad part of this story is that this woman's adult children never believed her, even after my consultation. I have no idea how sick this chemical may have made this older woman.

Case 9 / Throw Lots of Money

I consulted a customer in recent years about ongoing seepage. It was another case of wet carpet and belongings in the basement when it rained. I performed a very thorough, point by point, consultation with photographs and diagrams. There were improprieties with exterior maintenance items on every exterior wall of the house. My consultation fee included the initial consult, a return trip to present my report and an additional visit to inspect the corrections that were supposed to have been made. I made the first two appointments but was never asked to come back to inspect the changes.

A couple of years after that consultation I learned that the homeowners had added an "aftermarket" waterproofing system.

The inspection I performed provided conclusive evidence that the seepage was coming from mismanaged surface water. This customer fell into the "throw lots of money" mind set. Sometimes people believe that if a large amount of money is spent the problem will be solved properly.

Case 10 / Common Sense

A few years ago I consulted a couple about their house that had ongoing seepage problems. They had already spent thousands of dollars installing catch basins in the back yard augmenting the existing weeping tile. I explained my service that included an initial evaluation, a return trip to present my findings and a no-cost option of having me return to inspect corrections I had recommended. I performed the first two appointments but was not called back for the third.

Recently I was summoned to the same house that was now owned by a different family. The house was for sale and a deal had fallen apart after a home inspector cited several concerns regarding water in the basement. The real estate agent that had the property listed explained that the current homeowners experienced water in the basement when a drain within an outside window well backed up during a prolonged heavy rain. She stated that the homeowners had no other problems with seepage.

One of a few red flags was the floor tile in two of the basement rooms. All of the tile was totally curled up at the corners and coming away from the concrete. The carpet, though not obviously stained, was extremely moldy and had obviously been soaked in recent times. There was also some particle board shelf units that were deteriorating at the base where standing water had been wicked up into the particle board.

My first comment to the Realtor was that if in fact the seepage or water problem was limited to a one-time incident the tile and carpeting should have been replaced after that incident. No home inspector, experienced or not, would ignore such obvious signs of a water problem in a basement. This house was extremely nice and otherwise very well kept in a high-end neighborhood.

After I surveyed the interior and exterior of the house I found that the homeowners I had consulted years before had, for the most part, heeded my recommendations and addressed the exterior conditions in a satisfactory manner. This is the reason the seepage problems ceased, until the window-well drain backed up causing water to accumulate in the well and ultimately run through the window into the basement.

There are a couple of lessons here. The first one being that after a home sustains damage from water entering the basement the damage should be corrected. In this case that meant removing floor tile and carpeting, disinfecting the floor and walls as needed. Then the walls should have been primed and painted with flooring to come as budget allowed. There is a strong likelihood that insurance would have covered some of that expense, if only the initial clean up. Check your homeowner policy.

Window wells in older homes are sometimes deep enough to allow for a large window in the basement. The bottom of these window wells is often concrete with a drain in the center. Having a concrete bottom allows rain to collect just like setting a pan outside in the rain thus the drain is necessary. The house being discussed was seventy to eighty years old so the window-well drains were suspect for that reason alone.

Case 11 / Simple Maintenance

The following consultation occurred just last year. The house was on the market and the sellers had not taken the initiative to correct seepage coming in at the front basement corner nor had they scraped and painted walls that were flaking from years past when seepage was a problem on all the basement walls.

My inspection turned up a sunken driveway slab at the front corner, point of seepage. There were also some underground downspout drains in the front that were unknown quantities. Though the seepage was only entering on the front corner I inspected the entire exterior of the house. The only other items of question were a sunken brick walk on the rear corner and gutter covers that were added in the recent past. My instructions were to fix the sunken slab first. Then, if seepage continued, disconnect any underground downspout drains and run downspouts on top of the ground with extensions and splash blocks. If seepage still existed in these areas it might mean that gutter covers were allowing roof runoff to overshoot gutters and seep into the basement. The easy way to determine if gutter covers are allowing this to happen is to inspect them during a downpour. Covers like these have a tendency to collect leaves, twigs, etc., especially in roof valleys. Roof valleys are areas of high-concentrations of water and if debris collects there it could cause roof runoff to miss the gutter.

Case 12 / Water Everywhere

This house had problems that were magnified due to the type of soil below the house. It was built in an area that was previously a swamp or low-lying bog with a clay sub-soil. As a result water does not percolate down into the ground quickly.

After a rain or snow melt water tends to hang around awhile, if only below the surface. As a result mismanaged surface water from roofs and hard surfaces like driveways will find its way into the basement before it can seep deep into the ground below the basement.

Basement seepage at floor and chimney clean-outs.

This is a fairly old house, built around 1920. Houses built around this time, around Detroit, tend to sit higher out of the ground than later homes with basements. As a result there is less basement below ground level.

The problem experienced at this residence was one of heavy seepage from all sides of the basement. The slightly unusual symptom was that water seeped into the basement from floor cracks before it came in at the walls. The floor was badly cracked leaving lots of opportunity for water to come in. The mismanaged surface water ran down the outside of the basement and under the floor until it became so saturated it could go nowhere but up through the floor cracks. Once the ground was totally saturated beneath and around the floor it came in at the wall/floor joints.

The fact that this problem had been occurring for so many years means underground tunnels in the earth around the basement walls were formed long ago and enabled seepage to appear in the basement almost immediately after the rain started.

The problem with the exterior was most common: mismanaged downspouts and gutters. Some gutters were missing over smaller bay roofs. An area at the side door entrance, from the driveway, had two problems. One was a missing gutter over a bay roof, the other was the low grade of the driveway area adjacent to the side-door entry. Not only was water collecting from the low driveway but excess water came from the bay roof over the area.

Case Studies

The solution was to correct downspout extensions, add gutters to bay roofs without them and excavate and re-grade the area at the side entry so that no surface water from the driveway came near the house. The homeowner recently purchased this home. The seepage has been going on for years which means the ground is completely saturated beneath and around the basement. It will take some time for the ground to dry out after all the corrections have been made and maintained consistently.

At the time this book goes to press it has been several months since this homeowner made the recommended corrections to solve her seepage problems. Although there have been many hard and sustained rainfalls, the homeowner has experienced zero seepage as a result of following the guidelines set forth in this book.

Houses across the nation vary infinitely from one another. They are built by many builders, in various types of geography, over different periods of time and exhibit endless examples of abnormal or unusual building methods and situations. So, there will be exceptions to the common rules I have laid out here. Consequently one of these puzzles may be hard to solve by a homeowner alone, or in the first attempt.

I have found this to be one of the main challenges in understanding older homes. The inconsistencies and unknowns can be great. Factor in changes by an unqualified homeowner or contractor, through the years, and you can realize just how evasive some problems can be to solve.

PART III

SOUND ADVICE

The chapters included here offer additional education that can help better understand and reinforce The 5 Steps. Also included are unique situations that are important to understand as they apply.

- Permanent Exterior Plumbing
- Bad Fixes
- Aftermarket Waterproofing Systems
- A House Without Gutters
- Slab Foundations
- Septic Systems
- Drainage Ditches
- Other Issues
- House Shopping

PERMANENT EXTERIOR PLUMBING

From the inside of a house waste water is carried away by drain pipes. They transport water from sinks, tubs, toilets and washing machines away from the home to a septic or municipal sewer system. To keep our homes from being water-damaged it is imperative that interior drain lines be water-tight, free-flowing and permanent. Can you imagine the damage and unhealthy conditions that would arise if our kitchen sink was constantly leaking into the cabinet below? Or, if the toilets constantly overflowed? No one can live under these conditions. Yet, when it comes to the exterior plumbing of a home that is exactly what happens.

Houses are designed and built with the intent of keeping water out of the basement or crawl space. While gutters are not required by building codes they are usually necessary to keep roof water from running along the foundation wall and entering these areas. As mentioned in the introduction, I am challenging the building code councils to create a protocol for the *proper installation of gutters and downspouts* to help homeowners understand the importance of getting that part of home maintenance right. By not having a protocol gutters and downspouts are installed by anyone and everyone with the assumption that it is a no-brain project. It's just the opposite.

One of *my* goals is to emphasize the importance of making gutter and downspout installations permanent. This means that they would continue to operate during all seasons under all conditions with infrequent inspection or cleaning. As a result, they would not be a cause of basement or crawl space seepage or flooding. Gutter screens can be installed to keep leaves and debris out and not require any significant maintenance for two to three years or much longer.

Why has home building gone this long with so little attention paid to this house feature that has the potential to wreak havoc on our homes and lives? I believe the code councils think this area of home maintenance is addressed by requiring damp proofing or waterproofing of the foundation when the home is being built. But damp proofing may do little to keep heavy concentrations of water from roof and yard out of a basement even when a home is new, waterproofing on new homes is rare.

Permanent Plumbing Defined

per·ma·nent *adj.*

Fixed and lasting, or that which is not easily altered or impaired.

Maintenance of water around the exterior of the house is primary. All other aspects of the exterior, especially landscaping, are secondary. This means that a home and its yard should be designed, constructed and maintained primarily with exterior water management in mind. All landscaping, driveways, grading should be installed to keep water away from the house foundation without adversely affecting adjoining property owners or natural settings.

Permanent Exterior Plumbing

This quirky downspout arrangement is an example of a homeowner being overly creative to avoid ice on the sidewalk. Rates a 10 for worst downspout extension method.

Gutters, downspouts, drainage lines and ditches make up a type of plumbing system even if they're not referred to as such. By implementing and maintaining guidelines set out in this text these exterior components will remain functional year in and year out.

Before installing trees, flower beds, edging, patios, walks, sprinkler systems, decks and out buildings consideration must be given to how these exterior features will impact or inhibit surface-water runoff from the house foundation. This is easy to implement when building new. However, with existing houses there is often much that needs undoing to achieve the same results. For new home building standards see *Appendix B* where standards are set out that exceed those of current building codes.

The difficulty in creating ideal gutters and downspouts, making them permanently functioning, is not just undoing past poor installations but undoing any of the exterior features of a home that impede this proper installation. A home endures constant change from one homeowner to the next over many years. More often than not the focus is on making the yard look good with little concern for downspout location or performance.

Once water starts entering the basement there is little time, it seems, for analyzing exterior features in detail, although that is what needs to happen.

BAD FIXES

Clever Devices

I attach this label to all of those products by the home improvement store check-out lines and in mail order catalogs that guarantee to make life better in dealing with gutters and downspouts and to some ideas that have been around for centuries. In the **"5 Steps"** I provide simple instruction for correcting gutter and downspout problems. I recommend standard gutter and downspout materials. Here are some not-so-standard products that can interfere with having a permanently functioning exterior plumbing system and dry basement or crawl space.

This downspout extension gadget is awful in every way.
It's unreliable, flimsy and cannot work with a splash block.

Downspout Extension Gadgets

Types include: fold-down plastic extension that is open on top; corrugated flexible hoses; roll-out plastic tubes; extensions that can change angles; any type extension that is not permanently attached to the downspout elbow.

Bad Fixes

Rain Diverter

This device is comprised of a series of fins that attach to the roof eave. It disperses roof runoff like rain drops instead of a steady flow of water, that in turn is more apt to be evenly absorbed in the ground. They may be acceptable in lieu of gutters if the house roof has no valleys, the soil around the house is sand, the elevation

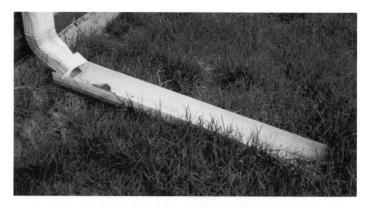

A downspout extension gadget, plastic folding tray, is not sturdy. Low grade and missing splash block are also a problem.

of the property slopes well away from the house, there are wide overhangs and there is no prior history of seepage. Discontinue use if dampness or efflorescence of any kind appears on basement walls, and install gutters.

One of many downspout extension gadgets. Not recommended because it's not permanent and has no splash block.

Gutter Covers

Covers designed to keep leaves and debris out of gutters may cause roof water to overrun gutters in heavy downpours, allow debris to collect on them if only in the valley areas, and do not offer a guarantee against basement seepage caused by overshooting water. Solid gutter covers may be prone to both problems. *See page 113 for more information.*

Gutter Gadgets

Screens, or other devices, inside a gutter at downspout outlets that keep debris from entering downspouts, in turn can cause gutter backup and overflow.

Rain Barrels

These have a limited capacity and can fill quickly and overflow if not kept drained. While I believe in water conservation and the benefits of rain water, using rain barrels can result in water entering the home if overflow occurs. If you're going to use them have several in tandem or an overflow pipe and hose to drain water off to a distant location. If you live in an area with moderate to heavy precipitation rain barrels might not be reliable. *See page 114 for photo.*

Cisterns

Underground or above ground holding tanks for roof runoff may be acceptable when the tanks are large enough to ensure against overflow. The pipes connecting downspouts to cisterns must also be free-flowing at all times and have watertight connections. Cisterns should have an overflow and cover to protect children, pets and wild animals from falling in and drowning.

Gutter Chains

Chains are universally accepted as effective ways to empty gutters in place of downspouts without the chance of debris clogging them. They are found more often outside the U.S. They are only reliable if they are not impaired by trees and shrubs, are installed correctly and empty onto concrete splash blocks that extend 36-42" away from house foundation. *See page 114 for photo.*

Interior Sealers

There are a lot of products on the market that when applied to basement interior walls are supposed to keep seepage out, however water must be kept out by sealing the exterior of walls. By putting sealers at the interior side water still sits outside the wall, inside concrete block and can get between the interior sealant and the concrete wall. Water will likely find another way to come in if a wall is sealed from the inside. It may come in at the bottom of the wall where it meets the floor or it may travel under the floor and come up through a floor crack. It can even go around the corner of the outside wall and find another entry point like a window or chimney clean out.

Sealants applied to the inside of basement walls are acceptable if water is first remedied from the outside. The benefit is to give a coating to the concrete that can help reduce condensation, efflorescence and mildew. The only product necessary to seal the interior of concrete basement walls is a good quality, *environmentally safe,* masonry primer and paint, again, after the exterior water issues are resolved.

Misconceptions

The most common misconception about keeping water out of the basement is that if it's present it must mean something is wrong that will cost a lot of money to fix. And right along with that is the misconception that if I, the homeowner, spend a whole lot of money towards this water problem then my life will be wonderful and I won't have to lift a finger to maintain the exterior of my house and gutters again.

I can understand being unnerved by water getting into the living space. That has to be the number one complaint of any homeowner, whether it's through the roof or basement wall. Water means trouble, expense and unhealthy conditions. But like roof leaks, dealing with basement seepage is about education and taking the time to

Bad Fixes

determine what one is up against. As far as spending thousands of dollars thinking that is a panacea, think again. Installing products or systems with a building permit, using approved methods, still won't guarantee and assure the problem will go away. Even if the problem subsides, side effects from some remedies can still occur. Some side effects might not surface for months or years. They can include environmental hazards to your family or damage to the house foundation and structure.

There is a common piece of advice going around that I believe was initiated largely by home inspectors. That is that by raising the grade around the *entire perimeter* of the house you can effectively alleviate basement seepage. The problem with this remedy is that it's not specific enough. Raising the grade around areas of the foundation that have no roof runoff, downspouts or have poorly pitched slabs will have little effect on seepage. It is important to have a grade sloping away from the foundation in areas where runoff water exists. To think that just raising the grade as a solution is wrong. Level grades, or even grades that slant slightly towards the house shouldn't be enough in and of themselves to cause seepage. Rain is absorbed evenly into the soil if no concentrations of water or unusual conditions exist. This generic warning takes focus away from the specific problem areas.

Yards with extremely low areas or holes that collect rain water, especially when no vegetation exists or in transitional seasons when the ground is frozen should have the grade raised.

AFTERMARKET WATERPROOFING SYSTEMS

Defined

These types of products, installed long after a home has been built, come in many varieties, installed by various companies across the country.

The array of systems includes: those with plastic panels against the interior of the basement walls combined with new drain lines buried beneath the floor next to the wall panels; drain lines alone buried beneath the basement floor near outside walls; trenches filled with gravel beneath the basement floor at outside walls; and every combination of the above. Some of these are referred to as "French drains." A sump, or basin, with a pump is often included with these systems to pump water up and out.

Why have these products come about? People with wet basements have had no where to turn to help solve their problem except companies offering aftermarket waterproofing. I make the distinction of aftermarket because waterproofing is generally part of the home-building process. Normally, a new basement is damp proofed that provides minimal protection against foundation seepage. Waterproofing is called for when building a new home if the basement is in an area with a high water table or for some reason the local building authority requires it, regardless.

This basement has an aftermarket waterproofing system. The plastic panels on the wall are designed to capture water between the panels and walls and channel it down beneath the floor. The floor has been cut away, a drain pipe buried beneath and the concrete replaced.

Aftermarket Waterproofing Systems

Scenario: A house is built thirty years ago constructed with damp proof protection. Over the years the homeowners begin to experience water coming into the basement during rainy periods or snow melts. They talk to neighbors or the handyman and aren't able to come up with a solution that stops the flow of water. Their next step often is to call an aftermarket waterproofing contractor.

Comparisons

Certain contractors only repair the existing drain tile around the *exterior* of the house. They are basement, or foundation, contractors. Their job entails digging up the earth all the way around the exterior of the basement, as accessible, and inspecting, repairing or replacing the weeping tile. They usually will re-coat the foundation wall with a damp proofing or maybe even a waterproofing product. Waterproofing costs more. The earth is then returned to the foundation wall. One problem with this method is that over many years landscaping, patios, driveways and sidewalks have been added that limit the ability to dig up the grade all the way around the house, or at enormous expense.

It is for this reason that homeowners often turn to companies that provide aftermarket waterproofing systems that do not repair original weeping tile to the house but instead install secondary or auxiliary systems at the interior of the basement. Keep in mind with either original weeping tile repair or secondary drain system the focus is not placed on correcting exterior maintenance conditions around the house that will likely alleviate the problem.

Approval

Some of the aftermarket systems may be *evaluated* by building code council evaluation services, or an equivalent, such as a local building authority. This is not an approval. Evaluation services may be an arm of a building code council responsible for regulating building codes around the country. For a fee they will evaluate various products to deem whether or not they meet some type of criteria. In my opinion, the criteria should be consistent with the building codes for new construction, but aren't always.

For an aftermarket system, in the case of one product, holes are drilled through the basement wall, concrete block or poured concrete, to allow static water within concrete blocks or against the outside wall to enter the basement. This water is then collected by plastic panels that have been added to the interior basement wall. The plastic panels channel the water down to the floor where a drain pipe has been installed beneath the concrete. This pipe may be installed around the perimeter of the room, along one wall or a portion of a wall. The pipe empties into a sump where it is pumped back outside or into a pipe that runs to a drainage ditch, sewer or dry well. Any of these systems have the potential to adversely affect the house foundation and home environment, therefore, they should be approved by an architect or structural engineer before installation.

I spoke to a local building official about how they go about approving such systems. The official is a building inspector for a municipality in Oakland County, Michigan. The city has one of the highest average incomes in this part of the country. This is what he told me.

Their building department has no official way to determine the quality of aftermarket waterproofing systems. They don't approve each system based on an engineer's or architect's review and assessment. He said that since the city doesn't have a big problem with residents coming after the building department for problems resulting from such installations, they don't scrutinize aftermarket waterproofing in a technical way.

Concerns

I am concerned about this method of drilling holes in the walls and adding plastic panels for a few reasons. I don't believe holes should be drilled in foundation walls to deal with basement seepage. I think it's a poor way to deal with the problem. Will the concrete become weak? Possibly, maybe not for years. But using the foundation wall as a conduit for water clearly contradicts standards set out by building codes for new construction, and common sense.

Secondly, plastic panel systems have not been approved from an environmental standpoint by a regulatory agency of any kind. As a consultant I have had concerns about these types of panels for many years as breeding grounds for mold and bacteria. Picture this: panels applied against the basement walls that are designed to collect water on a regular basis, water and dampness trapped between the basement wall and the panel that is always a dark space. How often does it dry out? It varies widely but just the fact that its purpose is to collect water whenever there is precipitation means the dampness might never subside. If so, there is certain to be a high percentage of time when there is water or moisture present behind these panels.

The point is simple. These systems have not been studied or approved for environmental impact. The potential for mold contamination of the home environment is unknown at best, highly unhealthy at worst. We know mold can grow on basically any substrate, including concrete. If the concrete is dirty, painted or has efflorescence then conditions for the proliferation of mold are greater yet. The consequences of mold contamination can range from allergic reactions to asthma to possibly a legionnaires-type illness or other unknown, so there is a lot at risk. There is no shortage of authoritative sources documenting this mold proliferation risk from this type of system.

Another gamble with these products if not installed properly, by a qualified crew, or using an approved method, is the potential to undermine the house foundation. For instance, if a system encourages surface water to come into the basement by passing beneath the footing, it can severely undermine the foundation over time. These types of systems are not designed to differentiate surface water from ground water, so it is unavoidable to prevent this kind of damage when surface water finds its way under the footing.

Finally, I have a problem with these types of aftermarket waterproofing systems because of the lack of attention paid to exterior building maintenance. From my experience little to no effort is made by these companies to inform homeowners about maintenance issues that relate to ongoing basement seepage problems. I am speaking about information that goes beyond "clean your gutters and have a splash block at your downspout." Even then these suggestions, if given at all, are done so in a very vague manner. Let's face it, these contractors are not consultants looking to educate the customer on keeping water away from the house foundation. Though they may be striving to dry up the customer's basement, they are looking to do so by selling their product. The goal must be: avoid wet or damp basement walls at the exterior.

Options

I don't think an interior-installed aftermarket waterproofing system is the answer based on my experience. If a high water table has come about since the house was built then some expensive action could be necessary; that doesn't mean one of these systems. Talking of common seepage from precipitation, i.e. surface water runoff, exterior maintenance is the solution. For those trying to avoid any exterior maintenance such as cleaning and repairing gutters I suggest you contact a foundation or basement contractor and have your basement fully waterproofed from the exterior and then make sure that no other features of the house will suffer from lack of gutters or other neglected exterior maintenance that normally keeps water away from the foundation.

Water coming up through cracks in a basement floor is not an indication of a high water table. It is extremely common to have surface water find its way under the basement floor before seeping inside. For houses that have had this problem for years it will take some time for this saturated ground to dry out, once corrections are made to keep surface water away from the house foundation.

A HOUSE WITHOUT GUTTERS

Over the years I've inspected many homes that were newly built. Most often these were the times I found houses without gutters. Sometimes the homeowner would install them down the road or in some cases a high-end builder had *waterproofed* the basement, ensuring against seepage from surface water. Many condominium communities, I've noticed, lack them.

This house has no gutters. It is likely not a problem because it is on a slab foundation and the roof has decent overhangs.

Here are examples of when gutters can be left off of a house.

Waterproofed Foundation

If a house has been built with a truly waterproofed foundation, versus damp proofed, it may be o.k. for gutters to be left off. Waterproofing totally encapsulates the basement walls allowing any water from the surface to reach the weeping tile and in turn drain away from the house.

Elevated On Sand

In some locations there are vast deposits of sand. If a house is perched on a knoll or terrace and it is constructed on a solid deposit of sand and/or gravel it may be possible to avoid gutters. The biggest concentration of water off of a roof comes at the valleys. The foundation walls below are the likely areas seepage will occur first if gutters are left off, even on sand. There is no assurance that seepage won't occur if a house is on a sandy crest. The type, age and quality of the foundation, along with overhang widths, are other determining factors.

Specific Roof Types

Roofs with wide overhangs that have no valleys, such as a simple rectangular gable or hip roof with no appendages may be no-gutter candidates. But again there are other considerations. Soil type, elevation, construction quality will all bear on the capacity of water to stay away and out of the basement, even with simple roofs. Even if no water enters the basement, interior walls can become damp when water rests outside them. This is not desirable.

Rain Diverter

A rain diverter is a device used in place of a gutter. It is a series of metal fins that is attached at the roof eave to disperse roof runoff. It breaks up the water so that instead of a steady flow or sheet of water running off of a roof a shower effect is created. These diverters work well along eaves but in valleys heavy concentrations of roof runoff are still an issue. Rain diverters may be ideal for simple rectangular roofs for houses built on a rise especially with sandy soil. There is still potential for debris to collect on the diverter but not as much a problem as with gutter debris and function. They may also be appropriate for houses built on slabs, crawl space foundations or with sharply sloping grade around the entire house.

Beware, even if a basement is protected against seepage when gutters are left off, there may be negative affects to the siding, trim, windows or doors. Houses without overhangs should have gutters.

SLAB FOUNDATIONS

A house built on a slab is one type of foundation. It can be on grade or elevated above grade. Here in Michigan, houses built on slabs are most commonly constructed when the land area is too wet for a basement or crawl space. The nineteen fifties and sixties were a boon time for ranch homes on slabs but they are seldom built here now.

When I was born we lived in a brand-new tract housing project built after World War II. Ninety-nine percent of the houses were on slabs. The area was a drained swamp. Our front door was just a few inches above the ground. When it rained long and hard our front-yard ditches were overflowing, luckily never high enough to flood houses.

One of the unique features of some of the slab houses around here is the type of heating system used. Many times houses built on slabs had heat ducts, for forced-air heat, buried beneath the concrete slab. If you combine this feature with the fact that many slab homes were built in areas with very wet ground you can see the problem. During certain wet conditions water would seep into these ducts and become stagnant. Very unhealthy conditions resulted. As a result I'm sure people have developed asthma and other respiratory problems. Think about infants living in houses with constant high humidity, mold and bacteria counts.

Typical post-war ranch house built with a slab-on-grade foundation.

Slab Foundations

Fortunately, the house I grew up in had heat ducts that came down the wall from the attic, never reaching the slab.

The only remedy for a house with this problem is to install a new heating system and seal the slab where the old ducts and returns penetrated. This is a costly repair. But if not done and a sump pump and drainage tile are installed around the slab instead, residual mold or moisture in the old ducts are still a serious threat to good health.

By installing a drain tile with pump around a slab foundation without this kind of heating system, some relief may be experienced from high water that might otherwise enter the living space between thresholds and under living area walls. Locating a sump pump for a slab foundation outside in cold climates will cause it to freeze while locating it inside will introduce excessive humidity to the indoor environment presenting a new source for mold and bacteria. It is possible to install an interior sump pump that is sealed air-tight from the indoor environment and vents outside.

SEPTIC SYSTEMS

A system is comprised of a waste line that leaves the house and connects to one or more septic tanks. From the tank a line runs to the septic field that branches off into a series of underground drainage pipes that run out into a bed of gravel. The principle is simple. Sewage from the house runs into the tank. There, solids are separated from liquids that continue into the field. The field is supposed to absorb these liquids as they seep down into the ground. The perfect type of ground for a septic system is pure sand, or sand and gravel. In these conditions liquid will run through the ground as far down as this permeable soil type exists if the septic field is fully functional.

Septic systems may seem unrelated to basement seepage but there are some scenarios that include deteriorating septic fields that can directly cause seepage. Type of soil, size of system, age of field are some of the major factors. Seepage can be related when a system becomes dysfunctional causing continued saturation of the ground around it.

An approved septic system is supposed to be a given distance from the house, varying with local governing ordinances.

If the septic field becomes saturated and runoff from roofs and patios cannot be absorbed into the ground then seepage may occur. Even when all proper measures are taken to ensure proper management of surface water a malfunctioning septic system or field can be the culprit. Home-made or antiquated systems found at cabins, cottages, old houses, farmsteads and the like are likely to need replacing. If poorly managed surface water is present on sites with a worn out septic field seepage problems may be severe and cause health risks.

How To Know If Your Septic System Is Failing *

- Black water with a foul odor backs up in drains or toilet.

- Toilets flush slowly, even with the use of plungers or drain cleaners.

- Surface water ponds on top of the septic system drain field. This is a sign that either the system is not able to "breathe" properly (oxygen must move through the soil to treat the wastewater underground) or the system is overloaded with water and cannot accept any more.

- Green grass over the drain field, even during dry weather. This means the grass is absorbing excess water and nutrients that ought to be moving downward through the soil.

- Weeds or algae buildup in lakes or ponds nearby. The septic system may be discharging waste water and nutrients to this area rather than treating it underground.

* Source: Oakland County, Michigan Health Department

Septic Systems

The threat for this problem exists for basements, crawl spaces that extend below grade, and slab foundations with underground heat ducts. Seepage into underground heat ducts can be every bit as serious as seepage into a basement. I have encountered two houses with problems related to septic systems and basement seepage, one involving underground ducts. When any doubt exists, especially when sewage smell enters the home, a septic expert should be called to inspect the system. This is done by digging and checking for saturation of field and condition of all components.

The possibility also exists for a leaky waste line between the house and septic tank that may include a bad connection where the line attaches to the tank or a broken line. If there is seepage with a sewage smell at the basement wall near this pipe and especially during times without rain then it is imperative to have this seepage tested for sewage.

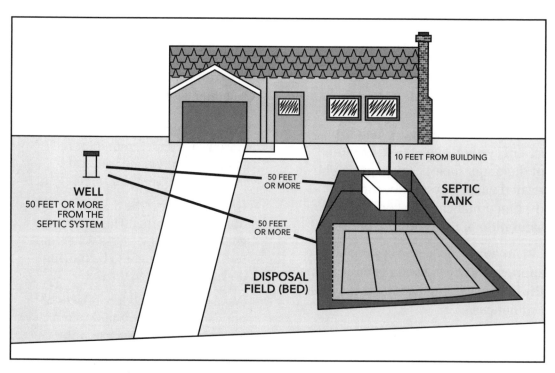

Septic systems distances are per Oakland County, Michigan.
Illustration provided by Oakland County Health Department, Oakland County, Michigan.

DRAINAGE DITCHES

If a home has a ditch at the front, rear or side property line, or through the property, it must be taken into account when solving basement seepage. This is a relatively simple matter to understand and remedy providing local authorities are responsive to homeowner needs.

In most all situations ditches that border property boundaries fall into an easement owned by local governments. Ditches may be part of the easements that exist for road construction, improvement and expansion. Where one lives determines who maintains them. It may be the county road commission, county drain commission, the township, city, village or state.

It is important to know that ditches bordering any property function in times of precipitation and snow melts. An inspection can be made under these conditions. Report any problems to appropriate authorities so that the ditch can be dug out, culverts cleaned or obstructions down the way cleared.

Drainage ditch not draining well.

OTHER ISSUES

The number of special situations that can contribute to basement seepage are numerous and beyond my ability to elaborate on here. Some examples might include: runoff from neighboring land, artesian wells or hot springs that bubble up without notice, areas in earthquake zones that may cause underground water to change direction, special gutter types unknown to me, unusual types of modern underground downspout drains installed by local governments, peculiar house designs, deceiving soil conditions, instances of prolonged severe precipitation, hidden cisterns, high water from hurricanes.

New types of foundation materials are introduced regularly. Some newer types include: PWF, or permanent wood foundation; panelized steel systems; styrofoam blocks; steel frame; stress-skin panels; pre-fab concrete panels and more. If any system is approved by governing code authorities they should perform equal to or better than conventional foundation types. They will be rated as damp proofed or waterproofed just like conventional systems based on site conditions and local requirements.

This book will serve to remedy most seepage problems if followed closely. But not all will experience complete relief, if for no other reason that people's lives are too busy and complicated to correctly follow all of the guidelines set out here. I know this from experience. Subtle defects are easily overlooked. Don't give up after the first attempt if you haven't made the water stop. Go back and re-read the chapter that most closely ties to the problem. Check your report. Get another person involved if need be. Use professionals as recommended to implement changes. All of the items outlined in this book are second nature for me. For others they may become a jumbled mass in the brain that might require taking a break for a week or two, then returning with a fresh and clear mind.

Certainly, after going through this book once, a lot of information will stay in your head. When returning to it you will be better prepared and have better results.

HOUSE SHOPPING

There are different concerns when shopping for a new house versus existing house.

New Houses

The focus for buying new must be placed on construction standards, warranties, existence of gutters and placement of the house on the site.

Find out from the builder what kind of protection is on the foundation. Is it damp proofed or truly waterproofed? Examine any warranties carefully to determine if the warranty covers repairs to foundation or plumbing if seepage should occur. It's also important to find out if damage to the home's interior is covered by such warranties. This includes ceiling, wall and floor finish materials and also personal possessions. Is there a deductible or a limit to payouts? Can a claim be filed more than once? More than once in a certain period of time?

Go over the finish grade with the builder with water runoff in mind. Examine slopes of yard, driveways, walkways, patios, etc. You can even check the builder's references of satisfied customers that have occupied new homes after a couple years.

Existing Houses

When shopping for an existing house it is important to be aware of basement or crawl-space seepage history. Aftermarket waterproofing is a sure sign of past problems, though not necessarily an indicator of a high water table or a serious problem. It does indicate that the homeowner was sold one of these systems and did not likely have, or seek out, another means to address the issue.

In my view, any house with an aftermarket waterproofing system that has plastic panels against the basement walls is an invitation for a high-bacteria or mold count in the home environment. These panels should be removed and the walls restored to their original integrity. You may meet with resistance on this matter.

Otherwise, when house buying it should be specifically noted by the home inspector what conditions exist outside the home that are causes of seepage problems, along with remedies. This book may be used to address items found on a home inspection report to determine how they need to be corrected and to estimate a cost for doing so.

Although common basement seepage may be easy to correct, there are exceptions. Houses that are situated on lots that are low-lying and cannot be re-graded effectively may be impossible to keep dry. Other conditions include additions to the house and landscaping that prevent proper maintenance of roof and landscape runoff. When a home has had serious problems of seepage over years there may be damage to basement interiors that requires gutting and starting from bare concrete walls and floors to eliminate mold and bacteria problems.

When it comes to crawl spaces it is imperative to have a thorough inspection of the crawl space and structure above the crawl. This can only be done from crawl spaces with adequate height for navigating. Therefore, homes with low or inaccessible crawl spaces should be avoided. Home inspectors are more and more reluctant to crawl around in these areas. They are often too low or wet and unsafe due to loose wiring and high levels of mold and bacteria. I would not buy a house without knowing the condition of the crawl space and structural elements exposed to the crawl, such as floor joists. These structural elements should be thoroughly inspected for rotting.

Showing this book to a home inspector will not necessarily meet with agreement or enthusiasm. It may be possible to take the home inspection report and make a list that can then be matched with items found in **Part II, The 5 Steps**. This can make it easier to comprehend what you will be up against as the owner of the home. It is also very important to hire a qualified and experienced home inspector. Don't be afraid to query him or her on their knowledge and experience with basement seepage problems. You can also ask for home inspection references. Ask for customers that have occupied their home for a couple years or more.

PART IV

ALL ABOUT GUTTERS

The following information about gutters and downspouts goes beyond basement seepage, though some explanations are redundant. Details are provided on certain products as well as how gutter system installation affects roof leaks and exterior siding and trim.

- Purpose
- Gutter Types
- Installing Gutters
- Downspouts & Splash Blocks
- Alternative Methods & Products
- Maintaining Gutter Systems

PURPOSE

Gutters are installed on houses to manage roof water. They collect the vast amounts of water from rain and melting snow and distribute it to downspouts that empty onto the ground. From there the water must be managed in a way that ensures its runoff from the house foundation, keeping it out of the basement or crawl space, or in the case of a slab foundation, out of the main floor living area.

Gutters serve another function. They direct water away from the house siding and trim, especially on houses without roof overhangs. I've seen two-story houses without overhangs or gutters experience leaking and structural rot from roof runoff that ran down the siding and seeped into door and window moldings. Over years of this condition window and door trim disintegrated, floors sagged and structural members rotted

This house has a poor roof design making this very ugly gutter arrangement necessary. There is likely a problem with excessive roof runoff onto the siding as well.

severely. In this scenario, houses with vinyl siding fare worse. Vinyl siding components are not a water-tight fit. Even when installed correctly water can get behind this type of siding. Houses with vinyl siding and no gutters are likely to have water and rotting over time, eventually causing rotting of sheathing, structure, windows and doors.

The bad roof design demands this gutter arrangement to avoid heavy overflow during rain.

GUTTER TYPES

There is a large variety of gutter types on existing homes and new types come on the market regularly. But the standard for new homes today is predominantly the 5" aluminum K-style gutter. This type of gutter has been in use for many decades at least. Before the 1970s the K-style residential gutter was predominantly 4", measuring 4" across the top, front to back. They were made of galvanized metal, previous to aluminum. There are many homes with these 4" gutters still in use. Other gutter styles include: plastic snap-together, half-round, gutters built into the roof, copper versions of K-style, plastic versions of K-style.

The aluminum K-style and metal half round are installed in either of two ways. One is to fasten them to the fascia board, or roof eave, the other is to use straps that are nailed onto the roofing. Straps are used on houses that have no practical fascia board.

Gutter installed using straps.

Cutaway of a K-style gutter.

K-Style

If you look at a K-style gutter you'll notice that the front profile resembles a piece of crown molding. This design helps the gutter look attractive and not detract from the house exterior. The width at the top of a new gutter is 5" from front to back, the 4" size now obsolete.

The K-gutter can be installed with several fastener types. Traditionally, they are installed with long nails or screws that go through the front edge of the gutter then a spacer tube, or feral, then the back of the gutter and into the fascia board. Now there are a few alternatives, installed from inside the gutter eliminating the nail showing on the gutter front. And again, there are straps that fasten to the roofing.

There are disadvantages to this method. You have to nail through roofing itself for an aftermarket installation that may cause roof leaks. The straps might also be visible and unsightly, depending on the roof pitch. They can, however, be installed prior to roofing. By fastening with these types of straps it may also be tricky getting a gutter to fit closely to the roof eave and function effectively. An alternative to fastening with roof straps is to modify the fascia with blocks of wood so that a gutter can be hung in a conventional manner. See a gutter expert for all gutter installations.

Half-round galvanized gutter hung with straps. Notice downspout outlet gap at gutter bottom.

Half Round

A gutter that is shaped like a half circle is more common on older homes and commercial buildings. I installed this type of gutter on an older house I owned so that it looked appropriate for the house's age. This gutter style has less capacity than a K-style gutter but drains better. Half-round gutters are more often held on with roof-mounted straps. They are available, like K-style, in aluminum, copper, galvanized metal and plastic.

Built-in

Many older and high-end homes have built-in gutters. This gutter is built directly into the structure of the roof at the eave. Typically a metal trough is fabricated and soldered together along with downspout parts when the house is built. The life expectancy of these gutters varies based on original quality of material, how well they were installed and the degree of maintenance through the years. The main disadvantage of this gutter is the damage from failure. If undetected, a leaky built-in gutter can cause a lot of damage to roof eaves, soffits, siding, trim, wall structures and even interior surfaces. It may be difficult to install gutter screen on these types. If this type of gutter is eliminated from a house, in lieu of a fascia-mounted K-style, changes will be necessary at the roof to cover the old trough and allow roof water to run to the eave and into the new gutter. Old built-in gutters can be repaired and replaced. It will take an experienced trade person to do the work.

Plastic

As with so many products today gutters are increasingly available in plastic. The ones I am most familiar with are the shallow, flat-bottom snap-together types. These are not very sturdy and have a decreased volume compared to K-types, making them inferior. The purpose of a gutter system is to provide the best protection against roof runoff. Plastic gutters can offer very flimsy support for ladders. Keep that in mind when comparing.

Installing Gutters

INSTALLING GUTTERS

I've mentioned in the previous text that I recommend gutters be installed by a professional, despite the fact that it is often looked at as a no-brain project. But gutters must be viewed as an exterior plumbing system, which is exactly what they are. Therefore, if a good-quality installation protocol is not adhered to problems will arise down the road, one likely being basement seepage. The following guidelines are reference points for a good-quality installation. A homeowner or unqualified trade person who takes on this job may end up with a poorly functioning exterior plumbing system and water in the house.

When Needed

Before gutters are installed it is imperative to survey the house and determine where they are needed. For instance, some second story roof eaves may empty onto the lower roof. If there are overhangs on the upper roof no gutter may be necessary. Also small roofs on bay windows or porches may be able to get by without gutters. If a house needs gutters, as discussed in Part III, install gutters at all roof eaves over a basement or crawl space foundation with the above exceptions. Areas where two perpendicular roofs meet to form a valley are crucial and may also need a splash guard.

This upper-roof gutter has no opening in the bottom for water to run out. Instead, the installer left the right end of the gutter open for water to spill onto the roof below and run down to the lower gutter. The problem with this method is the water running out the end of the gutter can, in heavy rain, run uphill under the shingles causing a roof leak. The correct method is to have an outlet coming out the bottom of the gutter with an elbow attached that runs downhill with the slope of the roof.

Slope & Fastening

The 5" K-style gutter is the preferred type and the inside mounting brackets are not only easier to install, with a screw gun, but are sturdiest and best looking. The slope of the gutter is also imperative to assure proper flow of water. It needn't be too severe. The fascia board can be used as a gauge to be sure it is sloping towards a downspout. If the house has a hip roof then gutters may encircle the house continuously. In this case the same continuous gutter is sloping in different directions towards downspouts.

No Open Ends

Over the many years and thousands of gutters I've observed I've often found open-ended gutters. Gutters on upper roofs that empty to the lower roof, where the gutter is close to the shingles commonly have end caps left off. The idea is for the water to spill out the end of the gutter onto the lower roof, from there into a lower gutter. The problem with this is that as the water shoots out the open end of the gutter it often goes up under the shingles before running downhill. No gutter should ever have an open end. The alternative is to have an outlet in the bottom of the gutter, preferably with an elbow attached that runs down hill.

Gutter splash guard located at roof valley.

Splash Guards

Two perpendicular roofs forming a roof valley create an area of highly concentrated runoff. Depending on roof size and slope there is a potential for water to overshoot the gutter at the inside 90° roof juncture, the valley. Splash guards are pieces of metal that fasten to the gutter to prevent this. These are very important when gutters have covers.

Seamless

Another advantage to having a professional install your gutters is the seamless gutter. It is made on site by a machine that can extrude a gutter from coiled aluminum so that very long lengths of gutter can be installed eliminating seams. This is the only way to achieve a high-quality job. For a gutter installer to be well-qualified he or she must offer seamless gutters.

A debris-filled gutter is actually growing seedlings. The open end is improper and the gutter should extend the length of the eave.

Installing Gutters

ANATOMY OF A GUTTER

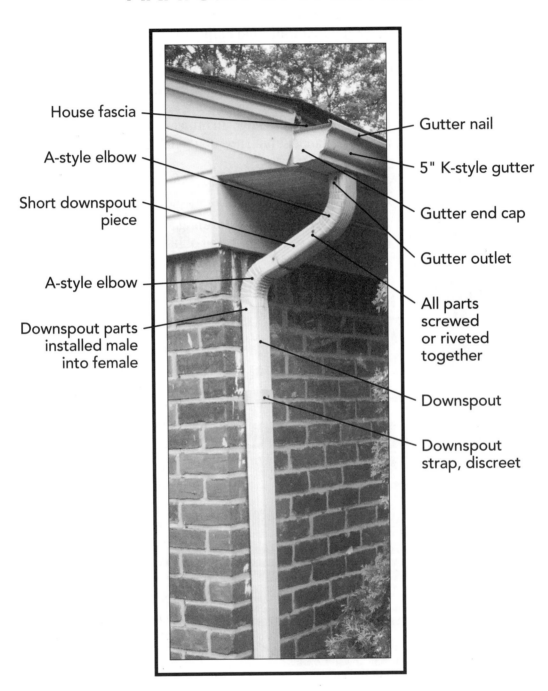

House fascia

A-style elbow

Short downspout piece

A-style elbow

Downspout parts installed male into female

Gutter nail

5" K-style gutter

Gutter end cap

Gutter outlet

All parts screwed or riveted together

Downspout

Downspout strap, discreet

DOWNSPOUTS AND SPLASH BLOCKS

Downspouts and splash blocks are addressed separately because of their importance. It is one aspect of gutter systems that is overlooked frequently. On all the home inspections I performed and on all of the "wet basement" consultations, the downspouts and splash blocks always needed attention.

How Many Downspouts?

A gutter contractor I used some years ago told me that the rule of thumb for number of downspouts is one for every thirty-five feet of gutter. I've kept that in mind through my many consultations and have concluded that is an adequate number for average houses. The need to increase that factor would come if the roof area running into that gutter is abnormally large such as on very large homes. In this case larger downspouts are also an option. Downspouts are also referred to as leaders.

Male To Female

Downspout parts go together male into the female in a top to bottom order. The upper downspout section, or fitting, slips inside the lower section or fitting.

Roof Downspouts

When an upper roof has a gutter that empties to a lower roof it sometimes requires a downspout. It doesn't require a downspout if the gutter empties out very close to the lower roof, within a foot. But the upper gutter, as mentioned above, does still need an outlet at the bottom of the gutter, and preferably an elbow running downhill with the roof.

The upper gutter has a hole in the bottom at the right end to empty onto roof. Ideally it should have an outlet and elbow running downhill.

Downspouts and Splash Blocks

The downspout emptying onto the roof has an elbow that improperly runs across the shingles instead of downhill. Roof leaks are possible.

This upper roof gutter has a proper outlet with an elbow that runs downhill.

The elbow on this gutter helps avoid roof leaks.

The elbow on this downspout is running across the shingles possibly causing a roof leak. It should have an elbow running downhill and beyond corner of brick.

Downspouts and Splash Blocks

Upper gutter properly emptying into a lower gutter.

Upper gutter emptying to lower.

Secure Together & To Wall

It is crucial that all downspout parts be screwed or riveted together including joints, fittings, sections, extensions and straps. Vertical downspout sections should be secured to walls with straps. They can be nailed or screwed to wooden, aluminum or vinyl siding. Anchors must be installed for masonry installations. Straps should be riveted to the downspout.

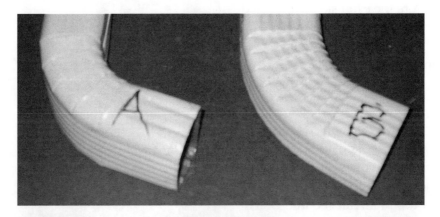

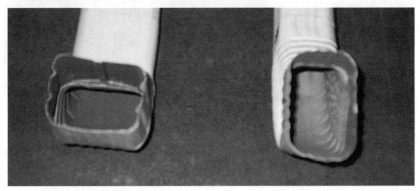

**Downspout elbow A on left for directing downspout in one direction.
Elbow B on right for directing 90° in other direction.
Lower photo is front on view of elbow end.**

A & B Elbows

There are two types of downspout elbows. The A style and the B style. They are similar except that the A style bends on the wide side while the B style bends at the narrow side. This makes it possible to turn or extend a downspout in any of four directions.

Downspouts and Splash Blocks

Downspout Height Off Ground

The bottom of the downspout where it empties to the ground should be a certain height off the ground to achieve a proper runoff. I have determined that the bottom of the elbow should be about 12" off the ground before the extension is attached. This will allow the extension to be sloped at a proper downward angle away from the house.

Extensions

Downspout extensions are one of the most overlooked and poorly installed components in gutter systems. They typically are too long or too short, too low or too high, not secured well or not fully installed onto the downspout elbow. Various gadgets are also used instead of proper extensions and are equally unreliable. Some of these include fold-down, open-top plastic extensions, flexible hoses, roll-out plastic tubes. There are also many

**A downspout hanging in mid-air.
Not recommended.**

homemade varieties of these devices. The only reliable downspout extension is a piece of downspout pipe about 18" long that is attached securely to the elbow of the downspout with screws or rivets. It is important that the elbow be inserted well into the extension end. With the elbow about 12" above grade the extension should be angled properly toward the ground.

There are situations on houses when the point at which the downspout empties to the ground leaves nowhere for the water to go. Such cases might be because of a poorly planned addition, a sharp rise in neighboring land, or a low doorway nearby. The only solution, if the downspout can't be relocated from the gutter, is to install a long pipe either fastened to the house wall or secured well at the ground to ensure proper drainage and consistent function. PVC is ideal for this but corrugated hose can also be used. PVC joints can be glued just like a drain inside the house to prevent leaking and joints from coming apart. Also make sure the hose or pipe is attached high up on the downspout so that it has no potential to back up there. This line must be kept free of debris and out of the way of lawn mowers and foot traffic and of course be sloped well away from the house.

This downspout extension is great. Good slope, distance from house and concrete splash block.

Splash Blocks

Splash blocks are another product that has become cheapened and compromised. Most all of the splash blocks I see at houses are plastic. These are highly unreliable. While we strive to make our exterior plumbing system, gutters and downspouts, permanent I must point out that this is another vital component to the equation. Plastic splash blocks get kicked, hit with lawn mowers, and believe it or not, blown away. Even if the splash block comes with metal stakes they are unreliable. The only reliable splash block is one made of concrete. Long ones are better. The splash block goes beneath the end of the downspout extension so that the total extension of the downspout is now about three to four feet and is sloping well away from the house foundation. Make sure the splash block is also at a downward angle. It is best to have the landscaping around splash blocks free of grass so that lawn mowers cannot disturb them. It is important not to have runoff impeded by garden edging of any kind. The water must be able to spill off the splash block and continue away from the house. It's helpful to pile some small stones at the base of the splash block to help disperse runoff and prevent erosion. Shredded bark is a good material to place around and beneath the splash block, as needed, to prevent weed growth.

Weed Barriers

Permeable fabric weed barriers and plastic sheeting that have been covered with rocks or bark used for the purpose of keeping weeds from growing up in flower beds are a major cause of basement seepage. They are unreliable because they form pockets and collect water. The permeable types cannot handle even low volumes of water, especially after silt has settled on top and clogged the holes. All weed barriers should be removed to within ten feet from any basement or crawl-space foundation wall.

Downspouts and Splash Blocks

Grade

The grade around a house is not always easy to change. For existing houses generations of landscaping and exterior improvements often create a difficult situation. Commonly, trees and shrubs have root systems that rise up out of the ground preventing a positive sloping grade away from the house near downspouts. If downspouts cannot be relocated the only option is to remove the plant. If the grade or house site is just low in general there may be difficulty obtaining any positive grade where needed, such as at downspouts. It is a misconception that the grade around the entire house has to be raised to keep basements dry. It is most important to maintain a grade that slopes away from the house foundation wherever there are heavy concentrations of water, for instance at downspouts, window and door wells, hard surfaces, planter boxes.

Underground Downspout Drain Lines

Many times downspouts are attached to underground drain lines to carry water far away. There are a few types that are highly unreliable. Old city drains typically made of cast iron or crockery are not reliable. Types installed in the sixties and seventies made of brittle black plastic pipe are not reliable. Drains installed since the eighties that are of the non-brittle cream colored PVC are reliable only if the fittings are still connected and they are not clogged. Corrugated plastic hose is good because it comes in rolls, eliminating joints, but the corrugated ribs can cause debris to collect and build up, impeding water flow. If there is any doubt as to the function of an underground downspout drain, disconnect it and extend the downspout as described with a splash block, at least until it can be determined whether this underground line was causing a basement seepage problem.

See **Gay's Downspout Extension Method,** *Pages 60-61.*

ALTERNATIVE METHODS AND PRODUCTS

Gutter Covers

There are many products on the market today that claim to save you from ever cleaning your gutters again. I think these products do a pretty good job of keeping debris out of the gutters but I have been told by three of these companies that debris can still collect in the roof valleys at these covers and I have a hard time believing debris doesn't collect on the covers themselves depending on the quantity and type of trees over the roof. If it is a low-pitched roof debris is more likely to collect. The bigger concern I have about these covers is roof runoff that may overshoot the gutter in heavy downpours. This is especially likely in valleys and with steep roofs. If this happens then basement seepage can occur. The benefit of a cover is zero if it does nothing to prevent basement seepage. So what if you don't have to clean your gutters. For those who already have covers and are not experiencing any problems I suggest leaving them in place.

Gutter system with built-in cover.

If a basement seepage problem exists where a cover has been installed then removing it is an option provided all other guidelines contained here have first been followed.

A recent study of gutter covers in *The Detroit News** reinforces my concerns about debris clogging covers, water overshooting gutters, and debris collecting in valleys and on gutters themselves.

Rain Diverters

This is another product that is designed to help save on maintenance. A diverter is a series of metal fins that attach to the roof eave, in lieu of a gutter, dispersing roof runoff so that it will be more evenly absorbed as it reaches the ground. The valleys are still prone to heavy concentrations of runoff. If you have removed gutters and installed these and are experiencing basement seepage my advice is to go back to gutters. If your home has wide overhangs, sits on a high elevation and has sandy soil it might be possible to use rain diverters. There may also be the likelihood of debris, especially branches, collecting on these devices.

The Detroit News, Column: Under Construction, Tim Carter, 11/06/04.

Alternative Methods and Products

Rain Barrels

Rain barrels have been used for centuries to collect water off of roofs. In the past the rain water was a valuable commodity and so the barrel served two purposes. It kept water from running underneath or into the house and provided another source of water. Today rain barrels are available from many sources. They are only beneficial if they are reliable. The main threat is that when they become full they can overflow. The only way to use these safely is to have an overflow system built in so when the rain barrel is full water is diverted to a downspout or underground drain line to carry water away from the house, as previously described. It's also possible to install barrels in tandem, greatly increasing the volume of water held.

This house has a gutter chain that empties into a rain barrel. Once the barrel is full it can overflow and cause a problem. The gutter end is also drooping.

Cisterns

This is another old world house feature. They serve the same purpose as rain barrels by collecting roof runoff but they are of a permanent nature. Cisterns have been installed in cellars, attics, above ground or underground outside the house. The same risks exist as with barrels. When the cistern becomes full it can overflow. I don't recommend cisterns inside the home because of the propensity for high humidity that brings mold and bacteria. Cisterns themselves can breed mold and bacteria. I would only recommend using a cistern for an auxiliary source of water for the garden. It should be a sealed underground or above-ground tank located away from the house and covered so that children or animals cannot fall in.

Gutter Chains

In some countries it is more common to use a chain in place of a downspout. When a gutter empties water onto the chain, connected at the gutter outlet, the water clings to it until it reaches the bottom. A gutter chain can be simple like a common link type or fancy and decorative. One advantage to using a chain instead of a downspout is the inability for clogging. A typical downspout pipe can become filled with debris, a chain cannot. A disadvantage is the potential for heavy winds to blow the chain, if not anchored at the ground, or blow rain off of the chain. The goal is for downspout water to empty to a concrete splash block for proper runoff away from the house foundation. The same holds true for a chain.

MAINTAINING GUTTER SYSTEMS

Gutters are held in contempt by many homeowners because they are always demanding to be cleaned. For homes with trees over roofs or in nearby yards gutters will need cleaning at least a couple of times per year. If the house is a two-story variety then tall ladders and hazardous work are involved. Gutter-cleaning services can be relied on for this. A better way is to install a heavy gauge metal screen across the top of the gutters. A gutter contractor can do this. If it's not installed securely it's of no use. By using heavy gauge metal screen, installed securely at the roofing and gutters, the semi-annual gutter cleaning can be avoided. Gutters and downspouts should be flushed before installing screen or whenever basement seepage occurs and gutters overflow. The best way to clean a downspout or an underground downspout drain line is to insert a garden hose with a nozzle attached turned on full. The brass twisting nozzle works well. It may also be possible to have a drain-cleaning service clean underground downspout drains that aren't free-flowing after using a garden hose and nozzle.

Copper gutter system from 1930s with soldered joints.

For gutters that have come loose from the house, additional brackets can be installed from the inside of the gutter that screw into the fascia. Leaky joints and connections can be sealed with a metal mender that comes in a tube. Be sure and clean the gutter well and dry it out. Follow label instructions.

QUICK TROUBLESHOOTING GUIDE

■ Gutters may be necessary at all roof eaves that run off onto yard. The 5" aluminum gutter (K-style), professionally installed, is the standard.

■ Make sure gutters are securely attached to roof eave, and slope towards downspouts.

■ Have at least one downspout for every 35' of gutter.

■ Downspout elbows that empty to yard should be approximately 12" above grade before attaching an extension.

■ An 18" extension, made of downspout material only, should be attached to elbow.

■ All downspout parts must be screwed or riveted together.

■ Downspout extension should rest on concrete splash block only, not a plastic splash block or the ground. Plastic splash blocks do not remain permanently in place even when they have metal stakes to secure them.

■ The ground at the splash block must slope well away from the house so water runs off and will absolutely not run back to the house. Examine closely during rain.

■ A downspout elbow with or without an extension may empty onto a driveway, patio or walkway provided the hard surface is sloping well away from the house.

**WARNING: IN COLD CLIMATES BE CAREFUL NOT TO CREATE
ICE HAZARDS IN THESE AREAS.**

■ Underground downspout drains must be functioning, with certainty that there are no broken, plugged or separated underground pipes. If in doubt, disconnect and run on top of ground as described above until it is certain they are not causing seepage.

■ Gutters and downspouts must be clean, flowing well during a downpour. Flush downspout by inserting garden hose with nozzle into opening at gutter and turn on full force. Flush underground downspout drains similarly. Use a sewer snake or professional drain cleaner if necessary to clean out badly plugged lines.

■ It is critical that either plastic or mesh weed barriers be removed to at least 10' away from the house foundation.

- Hard surfaces such as driveways, patios, sidewalks, etc. should slope well away from the house foundation.

- Yard must not have extreme low areas or holes that cause water to pool from rain or snow.

- Drainage ditches at lot boundaries must flow and drain well.

- Sprinklers must be functioning and directed away from the house. The duration and frequency of operation must not be excessive. Check for leaks at lines near house.

- The septic system must be functional, not saturated, with a recent inspection by a professional septic system inspector.

APPENDIX A
Soil Types Expanded

Boulders – Rock fragments larger than 2 feet (60 centimeters) in diameter.

Clay – As a soil separate, the mineral soil particles less than .002 in diameter. As a soil textural class, soil material that is 40 percent or more clay, less than 45 percent sand, and less than 40 percent silt.

Cobblestone – A rounded or partially rounded fragment of rock 3 to 10 inches (7.5 to 25 centimeters) in diameter.

Gravel – Rounded or angular fragments of rock up to 3 inches (2 millimeters to 7.5 centimeters) in diameter. An individual piece is a pebble.

Hydrologic Soil Groups – Refers to soils grouped according to their runoff-producing characteristics. The chief consideration is the inherent capacity of soil bare of vegetation to permit infiltration. The slope and the kind of plant cover are not considered but are separate factors in predicting runoff. Soils are assigned four groups.

- **Group A.** Soils having a high infiltration rate (low runoff potential) when thoroughly wet. These consist mainly of deep, well drained to excessively drained sands or gravelly sands. These soils have a high rate of water transmission.

- **Group B.** Soils having a moderate infiltration rate when thoroughly wet. These consist chiefly of moderately deep, or deep, moderately well-drained or well-drained soils that have moderately-fine texture to moderately coarse texture. These soils have a moderate rate of water transmission.

- **Group C.** Soils having a slow infiltration rate when thoroughly wet. These consist chiefly of soils having a layer that impedes the downward movement of water or soils of moderately fine texture or fine texture. These soils have a slow rate of water transmission.

- **Group D.** Soils having a very slow infiltration rate (high runoff potential) when thoroughly wet. These consist chiefly of clays that have a high shrink-swell potential, soils that have a permanent high-water table, soils that have a clay pan or clay layer at or near the surface, and soils that are shallow over nearly impervious material. These soils have a very slow rate of water transmission.

Large Stones – Rock fragments 10 to 24 inches (25 to 60 centimeters) in diameter.

Loam – Soil material that is 7 to 27 percent clay particles, 28 to 50 percent silt particles, and less than 52 percent sand particles.

Soil Types Expanded

Muck (sapric soil) – Dark colored, finely divided, well decomposed organic soil material.

Organic Matter – Plant and animal residue in the soil in various stages of decomposition.

Sand – As a soil separate, individual rock or mineral fragments from .05 millimeter to 2.0 millimeters in diameter. Most sand grains consist of quartz. As a soil textural class, a soil that is 85 percent or more sand and not more than 10 percent clay.

Silt – As a soil separate, individual mineral particles that range in diameter from the upper limit of clay (.002 millimeter) to the lower limit of very fine sand (.05 millimeter). As a soil textural class, soil that is 80 percent or more silt and less than 12 percent clay.

Stones – Rock fragments 3 inches (7.5 centimeters) or more across. Large stones adversely affect the specified use of the soil.

Subsoil – The part of the soil strata below plow depth.

Topsoil – The upper part of the soil, which is the most favorable material for plant growth. It is ordinarily rich in organic matter and is used to top dress road banks, lawns, and land affected by mining.

Source: Soil survey of Oakland County, Michigan, issued March 1982.
By: United States Department of Agriculture, Soil Conservation Service
*   in cooperation with Michigan Agricultural Experiment Station.*

APPENDIX B
Construction Standards & Codes

Construction Standards

Standards for new home construction, based on criteria set forth in this book, are to help homeowners understand and plan for proper placement of a house on a site and complete exterior work in a manner that will facilitate keeping foundations and basements dry through the years. Therefore the following criteria may exceed those set out by building code councils, i.e. International Code Council.

House Placement On Site

The placement of a new house on its site deals specifically with the orientation of the house in any one direction. The opportunity is best addressed when choosing a house plan. The plan should be chosen so that roof runoff is well suited to the site. Other considerations include placement of the driveway and how the site is equipped to deal with runoff from it and other hard-surface areas like patios and sidewalks. Selecting a site before a house plan is the best method for ensuring the plan best suits the ability of the land to handle runoff.

House Elevation On Site

Although local building authorities approve building plans for runoff conditions the responsibility falls on the builder and customer to ensure that the placement of a new home on a building site meets the highest standards for allowing runoff from roofs and hard surfaces i.e. drives, walks, patios, etc. to run away from the house in a very effective manner. Typically landscaping and gutters are installed after the building permit has been certified. Care must be taken to look ahead to landscape themes, and conditions that may change such as development of neighboring properties after the house is built. The worst mistake is to place the house too low not allowing for enough slope in the grade around the house. Placing the structure too high can be aesthetically unpleasing so consultation with an architect or builder/designer to ensure proper elevation is critical.

Waterproof Instead of Damp Proof

Simply put it is easier to spend a few extra dollars in protecting the foundation than in other areas of the home that won't be as appreciated in years to come. By waterproofing the foundation walls, instead of just damp proofing them, great benefits will result for a long-term occupancy of your new home.

Additional Gravel At Foundation Walls

In addition to waterproofing the foundation additional measures can be taken that are not required by codes or local authorities. One is to add more gravel around the foundation walls when backfilling. The gravel can be brought up close to grade allowing surface water to reach the weeping tile more easily, reducing risks of water seeping into the basement living space.

Compact Soil Well

To prevent settling around foundation walls, especially below driveways, patios and walkways, be sure and emphasize to the builder that you want extra care taken to meet compaction standards of soils in any area that was excavated and backfilled.

Landscaping

Typically a landscape design is not undertaken until well into the plan and build phase and very often well after construction is completed. By making at least a preliminary plan prior to starting construction, insight can prove invaluable as to potential problems regarding roof runoff and placement of downspouts within planting areas. When making a plan include downspout locations and if using underground drains design their intended locations and destinations. Take septic systems and drainage ditches into consideration as well.

Downspout Location Profile

Locate downspouts on a site plan keeping in mind the criteria most ideal for their placement. There should be no grass around the downspout but instead mulch of some kind. At the bottom of every splash block a pile of stones helps to disperse runoff without washing away mulch or soil. The worst maintenance headache is to have to cut the lawn around downspouts or splash blocks.

Construction Codes

Standards for new home construction and alterations to existing houses based on building codes vary from location to location and are most always at the discretion of the local building authority. The International Residential Code, for One-And Two-Family Dwellings, is widely recognized throughout the United States (currently 43 states subscribe to the International Residential Code). The following articles are excerpted from ICC (International Code Council), 2003 edition and should not be taken out of context from the entire code.

These examples are provided to help clarify some of the areas that deal with basement or foundation seepage. Excerpts have not been included that relate to wooden foundations or those made with styrofoam blocks or forms. This is a general view of basic codes, standards, for building new homes or altering existing ones with conventional foundation systems.

SECTION R102 APPLICABILITY
[EB] R102.7.1 *Additions, alterations or repairs.*

Additions, alterations or repairs to any structure shall conform to that required for a new structure without requiring the existing structure to comply with all of the requirements of this code, unless otherwise stated. Additions, alterations or repairs shall not cause an existing structure to become unsafe or adversely affect the performance of the building.

SECTION R105 PERMITS
R105.1 *Required.*

Any owner or authorized agent who intends to construct, enlarge, alter, repair, move, demolish, or change the occupancy of a building or structure, or to erect, install, enlarge, alter, repair, remove, convert or replace any electrical, gas, mechanical or plumbing system, the installation of which is regulated by this code, or to cause any such work to be done, shall first make application to the building official and obtain the required permit.

SECTION R106 CONSTRUCTION DOCUMENTS
R106.1.3 *Information for construction in areas prone to flooding.*

For buildings and structures in flood hazard areas as established by Table R301.2(1), construction documents shall include:

1. Delineation of flood hazard areas, floodway boundaries, and flood zones, and the design flood elevations as appropriate;

2. The elevation of the proposed lowest floor, including basement; in areas of shallow flooding (AO zones), the height of the proposed lowest floor, including basement, above the highest adjacent grade, and

3. The elevation of the bottom of the lowest horizontal structural member in coastal high hazards areas (V Zone), and

4. If design flood elevations are not included on the community's Flood Insurance Rate Map (FIRM), the building official and the applicant shall obtain and reasonably utilize any design flood elevation and floodway data available from other sources.

SECTION R202 DEFINITIONS *(excerpted)*

[B] **ALTERATION** Any construction or renovation to an existing structure other than repair or addition that requires a permit. Also, a change in a mechanical system that involves an extension, addition or change to the arrangement, type or purpose of the original installation that requires a permit.

GRADE The finished ground level adjoining the building at all exterior walls.

SANITARY SEWER A sewer that carries sewage and excludes storm, surface and groundwater.

STORM SEWER, DRAIN A pipe used for conveying rainwater, surface water, subsurface water and similar liquid waste.

TRAP A fitting, either separate or built into a fixture, that provides a liquid seal to prevent the emission of sewer gases without materially affecting the flow of sewage or waste water through it.

SUMP A tank or pit that receives sewage or waste, located below the normal grade of the gravity system and that must be emptied by mechanical means.

SUMP PUMP A pump installed to empty a sump. These pumps are used for removing storm water only. The pump is selected for the specific head and volume of the load and is usually operated by level controllers.

SECTION R404 FOUNDATIONS WALLS
R404.1.7 *Backfill placement.*

Backfill shall not be placed against the wall until the wall has sufficient strength and has been anchored to the floor above, or has been sufficiently braced to prevent damage by the backfill.

Exception: *Such bracing is not required for walls supporting less than 4 feet (1219 mm) of unbalanced backfill.*

SECTION R405 FOUNDATION DRAINAGE.
R405.1 *Concrete or masonry foundations.*

Drains shall be provided around all concrete or masonry foundations that retain earth and enclose habitable or usable spaces located below grade. Drainage tiles, gravel or crushed stone drains, perforated pipe or other approved systems or materials shall be installed at or below the area to be protected and shall discharge by gravity or mechanical means into an approved drainage system. Gravel or crushed stone drains shall extend at lease 1 foot (305 mm) beyond the outside edge of the footing and 6 inches (153 mm) above the top of the footing and be covered with an approved filter membrane material. The top of open joints of drains tiles shall be protected with strips of building paper, and the drainage tiles or perforated pipe shall be placed on a minimum of 2 inches (51 mm) of washed gravel or crushed rock at least one sieve size larger that the tile joint opening or perforation covered with not less than 6 inches (153 mm) of the same material.

Exception: *A drainage system is not required when the foundation is installed on well-drained ground or sand gravel mixture soils according to the United Soil Classification System, Group 1 Soils, as detailed in Table R405.1.*

R405.2.3 *Drainage system.*

In other than Group I soils (sand, gravel, silty sands), a sump shall be provided to drain the porous layer and footings. The sump shall be at least 24 inches (610 mm) in diameter or 20 inches square (0.0129 m2), shall extend at least 24 inches (610 mm) below the bottom of the basement floor and shall be capable of positive gravity or mechanical drainage to remove any accumulated water. The drainage system shall discharge into an approved sewer system or to daylight.

SECTION R406 FOUNDATION WATERPROOFING AND DAMPPROOFING.
R406.1 *Concrete and masonry foundation dampproofing.*

Except where required to be waterproofed by Section R406.2, foundation walls that retain earth and enclose habitable or usable spaces located below grade shall be dampproofed from the top of the footing to the finished grade. Masonry walls shall have not less than 3/8 inch (9.5 m) portland cement parging applied to the exterior of the wall. The parging shall be dampproofed with a bituminous coating, 3 pounds per square yard (1.63 kg/m2) of acrylic modified cement, 1/8 inch (3.2 mm) coat of surface-bonding mortar complying with ASTMC 887 or any material permitted for waterproofing in Section R406.2. Concrete walls shall be dampproofed by applying any one of the above listed dampproofing materials or any one of the waterproofing materials listed in Section R406.2 to the exterior of the wall.

R406.2 *Concrete and masonry foundation waterproofing.*

In areas where a high water table or other severe soil-water conditions are known to exist, exterior foundation walls that retain earth and enclose habitable or usable spaces located below grade shall be waterproofed with a membrane extending from the top of the footing to the finished grade. The membrane shall consist of 2-ply hot-mopped felts, 55 pound (25 kg) rolled roofing, 6-mil (0.15 mm) polyvinyl chloride, 6-mil (0.15 mm) polyethylene or 40-mil (1mm) polymer-modified asphalt. The joints in the membrane shall be lapped and sealed with an adhesive compatible with the waterproofing membrane.

Exception: *Organic solvent based products such as hydrocarbons, chlorinated hydrocarbons, ketones and esters shall not be used for ICF walls with expanded polystyrene form material. Plastic roofing cements, acrylic coatings, latex coatings, mortars and pargings are permitted to be used to seal ICF WALLS. Cold setting asphalt or hot asphalt shall conform to type C of ASTMD449. Hot asphalt shall be applied at a temperature of less than 200 degrees.*

Contact Information for ICC:
International Code Council
4051 Flossmoor Road, Country Club Hills, IL 60478-5795 • 800-214-4321

Permission to reprint the code information was provided by the International Code Council, as excerpted from their 2003 edition of the Residential Building Code.

APPENDIX C

Flood Management

What to do if basement or crawl space floods:

1. Do not enter flooded space. There is a risk of electrocution.

2. Call an electrician and plumber to facilitate a plan to evacuate water from flooded areas.

3. Determine if flooding source is from surface water around home, backed up municipal drain or sanitary sewer. Standing sewage presents extreme health risks. Collect water sample, making sure to protect skin and lungs from sewage and airborne bacteria, and submit to the local health department for analysis.

4. Call local governing authority for information on assistance for municipal drain problems. Inquire about insurance from municipality that may reimburse you for flood damage and expense.

5. Once water is gone and it is safe to enter area proceed to dry out space and furnishings.

6. Use wet vacs, dehumidifiers and fans to soak up residual moisture and dry out spaces.

7. Carpeting will need to be taken up to be sure it is thoroughly dried and cleaned, if it is salvageable.

8. Remove any finished flooring, wall and ceiling materials that have been soaked, especially if any sewage was involved.

9. Wash floors, walls, personal belongings etc. using an antibacterial cleaner. Be careful of moldy conditions that might cause allergic or asthmatic reactions. Wear rubber gloves.

10. Read all labels and instructions before using cleaners and equipment. Rely on professionals for all mechanical, plumbing and electrical work.

*The following information is taken from the FEMA (Federal Emergency Management Agency) web site (**www.fema.gov**).*

MITIGATION DIVISION

NATIONAL FLOOD INSURANCE PROGRAM

The mitigation division, a component of the Federal Emergency Management Agency (FEMA), manages the National Flood Insurance Program. The three components of the National Flood Insurance Program (NFIP) are:

- Flood Insurance
- Floodplain Management
- Flood Hazard Mapping

Nearly 20,000 communities across the United States and its territories participate in the NFIP by adopting and enforcing floodplain management ordinances to reduce future flood damage. In exchange, the NFIP makes Federally backed flood insurance available to homeowners, renters and business owners in these communities. Community participation in the NFIP is voluntary.

Flood insurance is designed to provide an alternative to disaster assistance to reduce the escalating costs of repairing damage to buildings and their contents caused by floods. Flood damage is reduced by nearly $1 billion dollars a year through communities implementing sound floodplain management requirements and property owners purchasing of flood insurance. Additionally, buildings constructed in compliance with NFIP building standards suffer approximately 80 percent less damage annually then those not built in compliance. And, every $3 paid in flood insurance claims saves $1 in disaster assistance payments.

In addition to providing flood insurance and reducing flood damages through floodplain management regulations, the NFIP identifies and maps the Nation's floodplains. Mapping flood hazards creates broad-based awareness of the flood hazards and provides the data needed for floodplain management programs and to actually rate new construction for flood insurance.

The National Flood Insurance Program, Program Description (619 KB) offers a more detailed overview and history of the program. Last updated May 29, 2003.
FEMA, 500 C Street, SW Washington, D.C.20472   202-566-1600

LOCAL GOVERNMENT

If a house basement floods due to the failure of a municipal drain system reimbursement for damages may be available from local governments.

APPENDIX D

Side Effects of Seepage

The side effects from water coming into a basement or crawl space are many. Let's start with the basement as there are some differences between the two.

The obvious effect of water in the basement is the possibility of damaging personal belongings and home furnishings. Over long periods of time continued seepage will also wreak havoc on the structure and finish materials on walls and floor.

A basement already has a tendency to get moldy due to the cold masonry walls having a low dew point, meaning condensation and residual moisture are almost always present. If the basement is well insulated and central air conditioning runs most of the time during warm months then this high moisture level can be minimized. Running a dehumidifier, along with air conditioning, or not, can also remove significant moisture from the air.

If neither of these systems exist the basement will likely have a musty smell. Sumps that aren't sealed airtight also introduce humidity and the potential for mold and bacteria into a basement and upstairs living area.

When seepage occurs water will be wicked up into wall materials and floor coverings such as carpeting. It is very difficult to rid the basement of the smell of mold even after carpet has been dried.

Mold commonly exists in various amounts throughout basements even without moisture and seepage problems.

Aside from the smell and the destruction of personal belongings and basement finish materials, seepage causes an even more hazardous condition. Mold has come to the forefront in recent years as an indoor home contaminant. I have been aware of this problem for many years and consulted with clients that were referred to me by physicians for mold-related contamination within their home.

Mold and fungus come in seemingly endless varieties. They irritate the lungs, cause asthma attacks and even illnesses such as pneumonia or Legionnaires disease. These many side effects should be enough to stress the importance of keeping water out of the basement.

In a crawl space the condition is often worse, not just because it is out of sight and high levels of seepage and moisture go unchecked. When fiberglass insulation has been added beneath the flooring from the crawl space side the propensity for mold and rotting increases. It is not uncommon to find rotted structural members in crawl spaces with continued seepage. The earthen floor that most crawl spaces have makes it easier for mold and fungus to grow and take hold on wooden structural members within the crawl.

Venting a crawl space will not alleviate these high levels of moisture. I've always recommended to homeowners with houses built on crawl spaces that they should close the vents, insulate the crawl space walls with rigid foam board, keep water and moisture out at all costs and, in cold climates, introduce a modest amount of heat into the crawl space during the heating season. Adding heat will help reduce humidity, dry out any residual moisture left over from the humid summer months, prevent water pipes from freezing and help create a warm floor for the living space above.

Insulation should always be installed on the foundation wall of crawl spaces and basements, not beneath the floor structure. Rigid foam board is the best choice for a consistent R value.

If insulated well with gaps sealed to prevent cold air from blowing in, the added expense of heating a crawl space should be nominal and the benefits great.

APPENDIX E
Side Effects of Aftermarket Waterproofing

I have two major concerns relating to the installation of aftermarket waterproofing systems in homes. The first is the conditions created by systems with plastic panels attached to the interior basement walls. The goal of these panels is to trap water, seeping into the basement, between the basement wall and panel and then funnel it down to a new drain line beneath the basement floor. These panels create ideal conditions for mold and bacteria to proliferate between the panels and basement wall. There is nothing to prevent these high levels of mold from entering the home environment. Whether the types of mold are disease-causing is unknown. No studies have been done on these systems, admittedly by the companies installing them, to determine their effect on the home environment and its occupants. At the very least it is a great unknown. The health and well being of you and your family is potentially at risk. One contractor of such a system told me they are exploring the introduction of anti-microbial additives to the plastic panels. If added they would only protect the panels themselves from breeding mold, not the basement walls. This is a good illustration of the concern even contractors who install such systems have regarding mold proliferation in home environments.

Aftermarket waterproofing can also pose a risk to the integrity of the structure. Unqualified contractors and workers can install systems improperly that can undermine house foundations and create extensive damage to the home. If systems are bona fide, that is, installed by a reputable crew and company, they can still, potentially, affect the structural integrity of the house. The approval process and scrutiny of these systems by local building officials is lax, from what I have found. Without the input of a structural engineer or architect the door is being left open for potential problems and unknowns.

Installing aftermarket waterproofing systems is sidestepping basic home maintenance. Letting water come into the basement so that it can be pumped back out again neglects a very basic tenet in home design, construction and maintenance: maintain your home to keep water away from the foundation. This is supported by current building codes as well as article after article from universities, insurance companies and independent home maintenance consulting firms addressing basement seepage causes and cures.

APPENDIX F
Mold and Bacteria

Basement

Mold and bacteria thrive in dark, moist, warm environments. By keeping moisture away from foundation walls you will avoid seepage into the basement or crawl space as well as damp interior walls.

Once this is achieved the next step to reduce mold and bacteria is to run a dehumidifier, fan and/or air conditioner during the humid months. In Michigan, once the heating season begins basement mold problems, caused by high humidity, diminish if surface and ground water are properly managed.

The only other potential for moisture is from a sump. I recommend that sumps be sealed and vented to the outside. This eliminates evaporation of standing water in the sump, that likely contains mold spores and bacteria, from entering the basement atmosphere. The added level of humidity into the home environment, from sumps alone, can encourage mold and bacteria growth to harmful levels. There are kits available, usually used for radon mitigation, that will seal a sump air tight and vent it to the outdoors.

To remove mold and bacteria already present there are several products available. Properly diluted chlorine bleach is most often recommended for this but I suggest a less harsh solution. Hydrogen peroxide, mild detergents, citrus cleaners, borax and any non-toxic cleaner that cleans household bacteria will work.

WARNING: ALWAYS FOLLOW PRODUCT INSTRUCTIONS FOR INTENDED USE.

Other ways to mitigate musty smells and kill bacteria include using an ozone generator, ultraviolet light or an anti-microbial fog. These should be done by a qualified professional.

Companies that provide these services deal with natural disasters like floods, fires, storms, etc. To locate one try the Internet or your homeowner insurance agency.

CAUTION: THE HOME MUST BE VACATED FOR SOME OF THESE PROCEDURES.

By painting, insulating and finishing basement walls mold and bacterial growth due to condensation can be decreased.

When severe flooding, high water or long-term standing water have occurred in a basement there is only one way to eliminate mold and bacteria. All of the finished floor and wall materials, below the water line, must be removed to expose the concrete walls and floor. If water has been wicked up higher than the water line by building

Mold and Bacteria

materials such as wood, drywall, insulation, etc. then this material must also be removed. It may not be practical to remove the bottom portion of a finished wall but if a suspended ceiling exists it may be less work to reconfigure the lower half of finished walls than remove all of them that, in turn, means taking down the ceiling. Remove any material contaminated with standing water that poses a risk of mold and bacteria. An exception could be ceramic or asphalt floor tile that remains secure after the flooding, though it will need a thorough cleaning and disinfecting. Vinyl tile and sheet flooring does not weather floods well, necessitating removal. Once all finished walls and flooring have been removed a thorough cleaning and disinfecting of foundation walls and concrete floors should take place.

> **WARNING: HAVE A LICENSED ELECTRICIAN HANDLE ALL ELECTRICAL WORK INCLUDING DEMOLITION, A PLUMBER FOR ALL PLUMBING MATTERS, A MECHANICAL CONTRACTOR FOR GAS LINES AND HVAC (heating, ventilation and air conditioning) SYSTEMS.**

Crawl Space

Crawl spaces can be managed similarly to basements with a few exceptions. It is not usually practical to run a dehumidifier in a crawl space unless it is very accessible, with a concrete floor. Crawl spaces built with a concrete versus an earthen floor will diminish the potential for mold and bacteria greatly.

I believe crawl spaces should not be vented but should be kept absolutely dry and well insulated. I also recommend crawl spaces be heated on a limited level. If the crawl space is part of a house that also has a basement and the access to the crawl space is from the basement then this access should be sealed to keep mold and bacteria in a crawl space from entering the home.

Crawl spaces are often at ground level which makes it easier to keep them from flooding. But having an earthen floor increases the conditions for mold and bacteria to take hold and proliferate. Short of pouring a concrete floor in this space it is recommended to put plastic sheeting, 6 mil thick, over the entire area, overlapping seams well, and then adding washed pea gravel over the plastic; washing the pea gravel will help eliminate dirt and debris that mold and bacteria can thrive on. This will keep moisture in the ground beneath the plastic and out of the crawl space. The better the plastic is sealed around the perimeter and at overlaps the less humidity from the earth will enter the crawl space.

Mold

Molds and bacteria are distinctly different living organisms. They both thrive in dark, damp and warm environments and feed on any organic matter. Mold is more apt to be recognized as fungi, i.e. mushrooms, or black spotting on shower and basement walls. There are many varieties, some that can be eaten or taken as penicillin, others that are deadly. It's not possible by visual inspection to determine if toxic or unhealthy mold is present. But, just the presence of mold on a wall or floor, or especially rotted organic material, is an indication of an abnormal and unhealthy living condition. There is no place in the home that mold is beneficial except for medicines and foods such as yeast breads, alcoholic beverages and mushrooms. Otherwise, in my opinion, zero tolerance is the goal.

It is possible to test for mold fairly simply but a more practical approach is to remove and or clean anything that is suspect of harboring it.

One of the more toxic forms is black mold that is commonly found on wet and decaying drywall, sheet rock. People who have no mold allergy are known to be affected by indoor environments with high levels of mold.

Mold is spread through a home's air by producing spores that leave the host, becoming airborne, free to travel with air movement within the home. They can then find new places to take hold and proliferate further, such as in a heat duct, cold air return or carpeting.

Mites can proliferate in a moldy environment as they feed on the mold spores. Their fecal matter feeds mold growth further. Spiders may become rampant as they find food in the mite population.

Bacteria

Bacteria, while different than mold, grows easily like mold. There is a wide variety of bacteria that includes types for fermenting foods and beverages from cheese to beer. There are also types that cause diseases such as cholera, diphtheria, ear infections, leprosy, Legionnaires disease, plague, pneumonia, sinus infections, "staph" infections, stomach ulcers, tetanus, tuberculosis, typhus, venereal disease, and many more.

While bacteria are necessary for life to exist there is a place for them, but not in the house. Unhealthy conditions are a certainty when basements and crawl spaces have seepage or high humidity that causes condensation and dampness. It is too difficult to approach these problems from identification of bacteria types; it is wiser to eliminate the conditions that cause them.

To live in a sterile environment away from mold and bacteria would diminish our immune system's ability to protect us. Therefore children, and adults, are thought to need outside activities where mold and bacteria are in abundance. Decaying leaves in fall or musty earth are examples. However, we don't need our homes to be damp and laden with mold and bacteria. That is simply unhealthy by any standard.

APPENDIX G
Drain Cleaning Tips

The sanitary drain lines in houses often need cleaning. Whether connected to a septic system or a city sewer, drains can become plugged. For houses with septic systems the line is typically short from the house to the septic tank. For city sewer lines from the house to the street, or main sewer, it can be a long run.

Older houses with clay crock sewers have a tendency to become root clogged. This requires a cleaning device that will cut through the roots and extract them. There are services now that specialize in drain cleaning and they may use a small camera to check the condition of the line. Drain lines within the home also need maintenance periodically. The cause may be grease build up, improper items flushed down toilets or put through disposals, poorly pitched drain lines, collapsed lines beneath basement floors, etc. Here are a few tips on how to best deal with a drain problem that may be causing seepage in the basement.

1. Try and assess the problem as best as possible before calling a service person. Make notes of the problem such as when and how it occurred. Give a history of the house as long as you've lived there.

2. Use only qualified people to work on your home. Call specialized drain cleaning professionals for serious drain problems, not a plumber.

3. Check references and most importantly get second and third opinions for expensive remedies. It's also a good idea to talk to neighbors, friends or local building officials about your condition before taking an expensive step.

4. Avoid using harsh drain cleaners in pipes. They're not only bad for the pipes they're harmful to the environment. Try less harsh products combined with a plunger and hot water. Accessible drain pipes can be taken apart and cleaned. You can also call a professional drain cleaner.

5. Have problem drains periodically cleaned before a major back up occurs.

6. Do not attempt to rent heavy drain-cleaning equipment to do the job yourself. It is better to spend a little extra and know the drain has been properly cleaned.

If sewer lines need replacing there is a method called CIP, cured in place. This uses existing buried sewer pipes and relines them. Check with local building authorities if this is acceptable were you live.

APPENDIX H

Resources

FOR PRODUCTS

I recommend professional gutter installation, but if you choose to do it yourself here are some tips.

The best place to purchase gutter and downspout products is from a wholesale house that sells vinyl and aluminum siding. They typically sell to the public. There are also stores that sell roofing and siding that should have an equally good selection. Either source should carry a variety of colors and hanger types for K-style gutters and accessories. These wholesale houses will generally make, extrude, the gutter upon purchase to any length you are able to transport and hang without damaging. These long lengths are called seamless gutters as opposed to buying several ten foot sections that have to be joined with connectors that increase the frequency of leaks and sagging joints.

Concrete splash blocks may be harder to locate than plastic types but should be available at hardware, home improvement and/or garden and landscape centers.

Corrugated plastic hose and PVC piping for underground downspout drains or weeping tile are available from plumbing supply outlets, hardware stores, home improvement stores and specialized commercial dealers of pipe, stone and related drain materials. Smooth PVC is always preferable to corrugated plastic hose.

Airtight sump pump enclosures, that vent outside, can be purchased through plumbing supply houses. Some of these businesses will not sell to the general public but might give you the information to find the product on the web and buy direct. There are plumbing supply houses that do sell to the public.

Window wells can be constructed out of treated wood, either 2x" stock or landscape timbers. Prefabricated units can be purchased from lumber yards or building supply houses. Do not confuse window wells with window well covers.

Six-mil plastic or polyethylene in rolls, for vapor barriers, is available at hardware stores or home improvement stores.

Washed pea gravel for crawl space floors can be obtained from nurseries or garden supply stores or sand and gravel yards.

Resources

FOR SERVICES

Aside from gutter specialists, gutters are generally installed by contractors that do siding, roofing and general contracting. What's important is that they install seamless 5" aluminum (K-style) gutters and that it's part of their specialty. (Having gutters hung by a "handyman service" is not as reliable.) These companies should install downspout extensions as described in this book if instructed to do so. If K-style gutters are not available in your area, subscribe to the standard of local building officials.

Underground downspout drains should be avoided unless an absolutely correct installation and performance is guaranteed. This may best be achieved by a skilled homeowner, an experienced landscape installation or foundation contractor or plumber.

It may be possible to raise sunken concrete slabs using a mud jacking technique provided slabs aren't cracked into pieces. Mud jacking is listed in the phone book or on the web.

Concrete slabs are replaced by concrete contractors or masons that do flat work. Asphalt contractors will replace or overlay concrete or asphalt drives. Brick or patio stone areas can be relaid or replaced by contractors specializing in that field; sometimes landscape contractors perform this work.

Low grade can be addressed by landscape contractors. Flower bed problems and window wells can also be dealt with by them. A general contractor may also be helpful.

Where to Find Supply Houses and Reputable Contractors and Trade People

Small-town newspapers in the Service Directory section of the want ads list contractors and building trade professionals.

Supply houses as mentioned above are usually happy to refer contractors that buy from them and typically have a good feel for reliable and not-so-reliable types.

Ask neighbors and friends about companies and people they have used for like projects.

Stop when you see someone working on a house that may provide the service you need.

Check references, licenses when applicable and ask to see someone's work if necessary.

The web is a very easy place to search for products and services. Just plug key words into the search window and go.

The Better Business Bureau may have a list of complaints against individuals but it doesn't mean that the person is reputable because they are not on their list. It also doesn't mean a business is reputable just because they belong to the BBB though it may mean another layer of scrutiny has been met.

GLOSSARY

NOTE: *Additional definitions may be found in Appendix A, Soil Types and Appendix B, Building Codes.*

aftermarket waterproofing – products and systems installed on a home after it has been built to help stem the flow of water into a basement, cellar or crawl space.

backfill – earth filled in around a basement or foundation wall after the walls are complete.

bacteria – single-celled organisms of the class Schizomycetes that are either free-living, dependent on dead and decaying matter or live within a plant or animal. They vary from nutritionally to medicinally beneficial to causes of disease.

basement – a masonry box in the ground that a house is built on.

basement contractor – a licensed building and alterations contractor specializing in basement construction. Also called foundation contractor.

block wall – a wall constructed with concrete blocks used for basement and crawl space foundations. Block sizes typically are 8"x8"x16", 8"x12"x16".

cellar – another term for basement used by older generations and often applied to older house types.

chimney clean-out – a metal access door to the chimney found in the basement near the floor that fireplace ashes are emptied to from the fireplace floor.

cistern – a holding tank found in older houses for collecting rain water. Can be located in a basement, attic, crawl space or outside.

clean-out – a plumbing access point for cleaning out waste lines for either city sewer or septic systems.

crawl space – an area beneath the first floor of a house that is too low for living space. A crawl space can be completely above grade or below grade. Not to be confused with attic space that is above living area.

culvert – a pipe used to let water flow under a driveway or road.

damp proofing – minimal moisture protection on house foundation walls to help prevent moisture from penetrating the living space. This does not waterproof a foundation.

downspout – the vertical pipe connected to a house gutter to carry water from the roof to the ground. Also known as a leader.

downspout elbow – a fitting attached to a downspout at the top or bottom to change direction of the pipe and to empty downspout water onto the ground. There are two elbow types, type A and type B.

downspout elbow A – an elbow that makes the 90° turn on the wide side of elbow.

downspout elbow B – an elbow that makes a 90° turn on the narrow side of elbow.

downspout extension – a piece of downspout pipe attached to the downspout elbow at the ground to extend downspout runoff farther from the house.

dry well – an underground hole or container that is filled with gravel so that water emptying into it from a drain pipe can be absorbed slowly into the ground.

efflorescence – the salts and other minerals that come to the surface of masonry walls after continued dampness.

effluence – discharge from a pipe such as a drain or sewer pipe.

extrude – to shape metal by forcing through a die. This is how gutters are made. They are made while you wait if purchased at commercial supply houses, or on site.

FEMA – Federal Emergency Management Agency that deals with flooding and other natural disasters.

flood plain – an area designated by the Army Corps of Engineers or FEMA that meets their criteria for high water during protracted periods of rain or snow melt.

flooding – the inundation of an area, caused by overflowing streams or by runoff from adjacent slopes. Water standing for short periods after rainfall or snowmelt and water in swamps and marshes is not considered flooding.

floor drain – a wastewater drain in the floor of a basement, laundry room, utility area, etc. to carry water away that accumulates unexpectedly.

footing – the concrete pad that a foundation wall or column sits on.

foundation – the combination of footings and/or walls that a structure relies on for support.

foundation contractor – a building or alterations contractor that specializes in constructing or altering foundations. Also see basement contractor.

french drain – an underground conduit for water comprised of a trench filled with gravel.

frost heave – the action of frost that can crack basement walls or raise patios, driveways, etc., as moisture gets trapped beneath or behind concrete.

frost line – the level at which frosts penetrates in the winter. Varies from area to area. In lower Michigan the frost line for building purposes is determined to be no greater than 42".

fungi – see mold

grade – the level of the earth around a house.

ground water – water that exists naturally beneath the surface of the ground. Levels vary widely from area to area and during seasonal changes.

gutter – a trough attached to the house eave that collects roof runoff and diverts it away from the house foundation.

gutter chain – a chain that hangs from a gutter instead of a downspout to carry water from the gutter to the ground. More common outside U.S.

gutter cover – a term that applies to a variety of contemporary products that cover the top of a gutter to keep leaves and debris out while still allowing water off of the roof to run into the gutter.

gutter screen – screen material installed over the gutters at the roof to keep debris out.

hose bib – the place where an outside faucet is connected to the exterior of the house.

HVAC – heating, ventilation and air conditioning as it applies to the building trades and mechanical contractors.

hydrostatic pressure – water that is under pressure and has nowhere to go, between a basement wall and the earth or a basement floor and the earth below. It can also cause clay soils to expand creating pressure against a masonry wall possibly cracking or bowing the wall.

in-ground heat duct – a heat duct that is buried in a concrete floor or beneath it. Some ranch houses built on slab foundations from the 1950s and 60s have them. They can also be found in lower levels of split-level houses and in basement floors.

joist – the structural framing member that makes up the floor frame of a house.

K-style gutter – the most common gutter style that is shaped like a piece of crown molding on the front. Older types were 4" wide across the top and were made of metal and galvanized metal. Since the 1970s they increased to 5" width across the top and are made of aluminum, galvanized metal or plastic.

leader – a downspout or water drain pipe.

masonry – construction material that consists of brick, concrete block, stone or concrete.

Michigan basement – a vernacular description of a basement typically low, under 6', with a dirt floor that does not continue beneath the entire first floor of the house. An old-fashioned cellar.

mold – one of the organisms from the fungi kingdom, that also includes yeast, smuts, mushrooms. Mold and fungi thrive on organic matter, some are highly toxic others irritate allergies and asthma.

mud jacking – a method for raising sunken slabs of concrete that entails drilling holes in the slab and pumping a liquid limestone mixture beneath it until it is raised back into position and facilitates proper runoff from precipitation.

municipal drain – a drain that carries runoff from rain or snow from city streets and residences.

portland cement – a product manufactured from a heated mixture of limestone and clay facilitating the production of concrete.

poured wall – a wall made by pouring concrete between two forms. The common method used today for building basements.

PVC – polyvinyl chloride, material used for making plastic pipe for plumbing.

rain barrel – a barrel used for collecting rain water from the roof of a house.

ranch – a single-story house, typically with a low-pitched roof, that came into prominence during the 1950s.

Realtor – the trademark name for a member of the National Association of Real Estate Professionals.

rod hole – a hole left in a poured wall after the rod that holds the forms together during pouring is removed. The rods can also be broken off and left within the wall.

roof eave – the horizontal edge of the roof where gutters are attached.

roof rake – the angled edge of the roof that forms a gable.

runoff – precipitation from rain or snow that runs off of roofs, hard surfaces or the ground.

sanitary sewer – the waste line connected to a house that takes waste water from baths, kitchen and laundry area and carries it to a municipal treatment plant.

saturation – the level reached when soil can absorb no more water.

seepage – water that trickles or seeps into a house at the basement or crawl space.

septic field – a large area within the house's yard that contains pipes for disbursing sewage into the ground.

septic system – the septic tank, field and leaders that are assembled to collect sewage from a home and disburse into the ground.

septic tank – the holding tank for waste solids. A system may have more than one tank.

sillcock – an outside faucet on a house.

slab foundation – a house foundation that has a concrete floor at the first floor with no basement or crawl space below.

slab-on-grade foundation – the same as a slab foundation yet is on the same level as the grade around the house.

spigot – a faucet, or outside faucet on a house.

splash block – a concrete block that is designed to carry water from a downspout farther out into the yard. Plastic splash blocks also exist but are not recommended.

splash guard – a piece of metal attached to a gutter when the gutter forms an inside 90° angle just below a roof valley. The splash guard prevents heavy concentrations of water coming down a roof valley from overshooting the gutter or splashing out.

split-level house – a bi-, tri- or quad-level house that has levels staggered over one another. Houses also exist with more than four different levels.

stoop – a small, raised front or rear porch attached to a house. May or may not have a roof.

stoop with basement – a small raised front or rear porch with a basement extending beneath it. May or may not have a roof.

sump – a hole beneath the basement or crawl space floor that collects water that in turn drains away or is pumped outside.

sump pump – a pump that sits in the bottom of a sump that pumps collected water either to the surface outside, into a sewer line or underground to a ditch or rear lot location.

sump pump check valve – installed at the pump discharge line to prevent water from running back into the sump once the pump shuts off.

surface water – water that collects on the surface of the ground from precipitation.

underground downspout drain – a buried drain line that a gutter downspout runs into facilitating the transport of water away from the house.

underground tunnels – tunnels created against the outside basement or foundation wall of a house caused by continued seepage through the years.

vapor barrier – a material used to prevent moisture from traveling from one area to another. In a crawl space the vapor barrier is placed on the earth floor of the space to keep moisture from entering the area. It is also required beneath basement floors in new construction.

wall gutter – a plastic panel used by "aftermarket" waterproofing companies to collect water against a basement wall and divert it to a drain within the basement floor.

water table – the level at which water appears upon digging a test hole. There are different kinds of water tables, see PART I, Water Tables.

waterproofing – methods and products used to keep a house foundation dry and prevent the conduction of any moisture to the inside of the house.

waterproofing contractor – generally refers to "aftermarket" types of waterproofing that can include bona fide recommended methods but also many systems and methods not approved.

weed barrier – plastic sheeting or permeable mesh fabric placed beneath bark or stone ground covers in flower beds to prevent weeds. Common cause of basement seepage.

weeping tile – a drain system designed to keep water away from the house foundation. It is installed while the basement is being built and is located at a level beneath the basement floor but not below the bottom of the footing.

BIBLIOGRAPHY

BOOKS

Ball, John E. *Light Construction Techniques: From Foundation To Finish*. Reston, VA: Reston Publishing Company. 1980.

Berthold-Bond, Annie. *Clean And Green*. Woodstock, NY: Ceres Press. 1990.

Blake, Earnest G., M.R.S.I., A.B.I.C.C. *Damp Walls*. D. Van Nostrand Company. 1923.

Dagostino, Frank R. *Residential Construction Handbook*. Reston, VA: Reston Publishing Company, Inc. 1983.

Dyer, Betsey Dexter. *A Field Guide to Bacteria*. Ithaca: Comstock Publishing Associates, a division of Cornell University Press. 2004.

Feenstra, James E., Soil Conservation Service. *Soil Survey Of Oakland County, Michigan*. United States Department Of Agriculture, Soil Conservation Service, In Cooperation With Michigan Agricultural Experiment Station. 1982.

Gay, Ronald K. *House And Home Almanac For Real Estate Professionals*. Pontiac, MI: Welkin House. 1993.

Haege, Glenn. *Fix It Fast And Easy*. Royal Oak, MI: Master Handyman Press. 1991.

Harwood, Barbara Bannon. *The Healing House*. Carlsbad, CA: Hay House, Inc. 1997.

Hobbs, Angela. *The Sick House Survival Guide*. Gabriola Island, BC, Canada: New Society Publishers. 2003

International Code Council. *International Residential Code*. Country Club Hills IL: International Code Council. 2003

Keith, M.L. *How To Build It*. Minneapolis: Keith's Architectural Service.

Lankarge, Vicki. *What Every Homeowner Needs To Know About Mold*. New York: McGraw-Hill. 2003.

Macaulay, David. *Underground*. Boston: Houghton Mifflin Company. 1976.

May, Jeffrey C. *My House Is Killing Me*. Baltimore: The John Hopkins University Press. 2001.

Maurice, A.E. *The Wet Basement Manual*. Addison, IL: The Aberdeen Group. 1993

Olin, Harold B. A.I.A. *Construction Principles, Materials, And Methods*. Chicago: The Institute Of Financial Education. 1975.

Peurifoy, R.L. *Construction Planning, Equipment, And Methods*. New York: McGraw-Hill Book Company, Inc.1956

U.S. Dept. of Commerce. *Care And Repair Of The House*. Washington: United States Government Printing Office. 1950.

PERIODICALS

Carter, Tim. "Under Construction: Cleaning Will Need To Be Done if You Have Gutter Guards Installed." *The Detroit News*. 11/06/04.

Engel, Andy. "All About Rain Gutters." *Fine Homebuilding*. Issue 125.

Janesky, Larry. "Keeping a Basement Dry." *Fine Homebuilding*. Issue 140.

Lugano, Fred. "Fixes for Damp, Moldy Houses." *Fine Homebuilding*. Issue 125.

Mother Earth News. "Harvest the Rain." 09/22/03. Adapted from the *Environmental Building News*.

Papa, Byron. "Draining Gutter Runoff." *Fine Homebuilding*. Issue 125.

WEB SITES

www.fema.gov
(Federal Emergency Management Agency)

www.gardenwatersaver.com

www.icc.safe.org
(International Code Council)

www.niagarafallslive.com

INDEX